AF326775

GO
PUBLIC
IN PRIVATE

GO PUBLIC IN PRIVATE

MICHELE HAMMANN

A Strategic Blueprint to Go from Owner to Investor

Go Public in Private
Copyright © 2026 by Michele Hammann
All rights reserved.

No part of this publication may be reproduced, stored in a retrieval system, or transmitted in any form or by any means—electronic, mechanical, photocopying, recording, or otherwise—without the prior written permission of the publisher, except for brief quotations used in reviews, academic work, or commentary, as permitted by law.

Edited by Catt Editing LLC
Cover design by Pete Garceau
Interior design by Zoe Norvell

ISBN:
Hardback: 978-1-966372-09-7
Paperback: 978-1-966372-08-0
Audiobook: 978-1-966372-28-8
eBook: 978-1-966372-29-5

Published by Author.Inc
This book is intended to provide general information on the subject matter covered. It is provided with the understanding that the author and publisher are not rendering legal, financial, medical, psychological, or other professional advice. Readers should consult licensed professionals for advice relevant to their situation.

The author and publisher disclaim all liability for any loss or risk, personal or otherwise, incurred as a consequence, directly or indirectly, of the use and application of any of the contents of this book. No results are guaranteed.

Printed in the United States of America
First Edition: March 2026
For more information, visit: gopublicinprivate.com

TABLE OF CONTENTS

Introduction

If your company were publicly traded, would investors see growth—or get out fast?

That single question can change how you make decisions, where you invest your time, and how fast your business becomes the asset that funds your freedom. It's about seeing your business through the eyes of someone who expects results. You need an investor's lens.

Nothing Seems Designed for Where You Are

You've built a good business. It could be better, but it's doing well. You understand that. You also feel like there's something more out there.

Nothing seems designed to help take you to the next level. You listen to the podcasts, and they're full of shallow euphemisms about how people built their business. You look for software as a solution, but it's just a tool. You get advice for people who are either in the beginning stages of their business or on the verge of total burnout. You sit through masterminds and Zooms where someone starts talking about KPIs like you've never heard of that concept before.

Where is the playbook for business builders, like you? People who've done it before. People who know systems that other people have used successfully to get to where they want to be. You don't feel seen in any of the business books you've invested time in. A three-hundred-page list of things that would be impossible to execute and may not have any value does nobody any good. And what if it just adds levels of bureaucracy, confusion, and stagnation?

You feel like you're constantly working on your business, trying to improve it, but to what end?

Growth at all costs is exhausting.

Nothing quite captures what you want it to be. And maybe you're not even sure what you want it to be.

Do you stay here where you currently are? Or do you take your business to the next level and grow?

Leverage the Structure of Public Companies Without Going Public

I'm going to show you how to harness the structure of public companies and leverage it for growth that inspires, not exhausts, you. You'll understand the valuation mindset and use it to make decisions that increase value and get you where you want to be *without having to go public*.

It's time to start treating your business like the asset it is. You'll see how it correlates with what's in your stock portfolio and why you should hold them both to the same standards.

You'll capture your vision of where you want to be. You'll look into the future and then build a structure that allows for accountability, scale, control, and bringing people along with you in the process.

Ultimately, you will also position yourself for an eventual exit or succession that ensures the legacy and continuity of your business, and you don't need to bring in the SEC as a marker of success.

The same practices that help a company go public will help you achieve all of this, without ever ringing the opening bell.

What You'll Learn

This is the moment you stop identifying as "small."

The instinct to push back on process, the part of you that sees structure as bureaucracy, will soon begin to fall away. In time, you'll recognize that the feelings of restriction were actually vision, discipline, and accountability.

Instead of dismissing how public companies operate, you'll start extracting the parts that can help you. The systems, reporting rhythms, and governance that create valuation at scale will become tools, not because "That's what big companies do," but because they serve your goals and accelerate where you're going.

Returns will matter differently—not just returns on equity, but returns on your time, energy, and focus. Your calendar becomes an investment portfolio, not a to-do list.

More people will enter your world. You'll delegate more, elevate others, and stop being the ceiling of your own business. Scaling becomes a shared effort rather than a personal grind.

Financial statements will stop feeling like paperwork and start functioning as strategy. Forecasting, modeling, and rhythm-based reporting will help you see around corners and operate with foresight, not reaction.

Failure will take on a new meaning. Rather than signs of limitation, missteps become data, learning, and leverage.

You'll gain clarity around the value drivers that separate you from competitors. The differentiators, assets, and advantages that make your business *worth more than the one down the street* will finally be visible and intentional.

Soon, you'll think in terms of valuation, not just revenue. You'll picture your stock price. You'll assess your company like an outside investor evaluating whether to buy in or walk away.

Your capital structure will evolve from convenient to strategic. Funding choices will align with the future you're building, not the comfort or short-cuts of today.

Finally, you'll create alignment and loyalty at scale by sharing upsides with the people helping you build—not as charity or obligation, but as a strategy to win faster and grow bigger than you ever could alone.

By applying the lessons in this book, you're going to build something that might be so fun, you never want to exit it. Great! If you do, though, you'll have a legacy that outlasts you, a true representation and a nod to all of the investment and work you've done as a business owner.

Why I Wrote This Book

I've lived both lives. I've worked inside some of the world's largest publicly traded companies and saw how they do business: how they interact, why they do what they do, how they have their investor calls.

Today, I own a business. I live it every day personally, and I have helped thousands of business owners take this system, and pieces of it, to transform their businesses and their lives, to create financial independence and leave a lasting legacy.

Business isn't just systems; it's mindset. I wrote this book for you, not for Wall Street or a boardroom. I've been in the trenches, and I know what it takes to build something meaningful. But to grow, you have to see your business differently. You must look at it the way an investor would, not just as the person operating it.

Structure and accountability aren't elements of bureaucracy. They create freedom. When you run your business with the same discipline public companies use, even while staying private, you gain clarity, confidence, and control. You understand what you have, why it matters, and what should or should not be prioritized.

Think of this book as the start of your advisory board, a tool kit, and a shift in perspective all at once.

Clarity, confidence, and control come down to two things: (1) how you operate day to day, and (2) where you're headed over the next five to ten years.

When decisions are made only in the context of this week, the business drifts. Long-term vision simplifies short-term choices because you understand their impact. You can adjust direction, but not every step is a reinvention. You're leading toward a defined destination.

By following this process, you build the structure and insight needed to pivot without chaos. If a buyer knocks on the door, you're ready. If your industry shifts, you're already ahead of it. You can confidently say, "If I take this path, my stock price becomes X. If I continue toward exit, it becomes Y."

That clarity is what creates real decision-making power.

That's the point: Strategic planning gives you clarity, clarity builds confidence, and confidence gives you control.

When you're done reading, you won't be tumbling toward decisions. You'll be getting ready for them.

All businesses start small, but let's reclaim your identity as a builder and an investor, as someone who's not just here for the moment but for the entire long road.

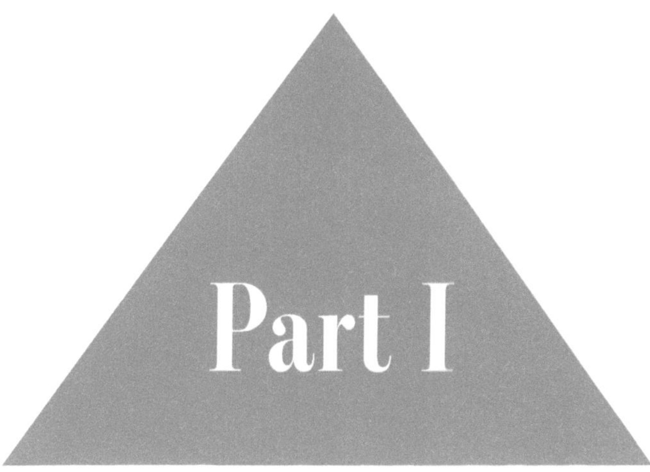

Think Like The Street

CHAPTER 1

Why "Small Business" Is A Dangerous Label

I've always considered the term "small business" as offensive to the entrepreneurs who own them and the people who work there. Your business might be small compared to Fortune 500 companies, but it's a big deal. If you don't see yourself as big and growing, you'll leave money on the table and underestimate your value and what you're doing for others.

The term "small" itself suggests unimportant. Yet the statistics tell a different story. Small businesses represent 99 percent of all businesses because they're defined as having five hundred or fewer employees.[1] That's not small; that's the backbone of our economy.

I sometimes rant to my girlfriend Kirsten, who named her podcast *The Small Business Mindset*. "Why, Kirsten? Why would anyone want a small business mindset when they could have a big business mindset?" You want to focus on the future, prosperity, and growth. *Small* is a limiting word that creates limiting results.

When people see themselves as small, they play small. You don't have small hopes or small dreams. You have a business. When you view it through the lens of limitation, you underestimate the value you bring to the world, your team, and your family as you work to increase your business's impact.

---

1   "Frequently Asked questions About Small Business, 2024," Advocacy.sba.gov, July 23, 2024, https://advocacy.sba.gov/2024/07/23/frequently-asked-questions-about-small-business-2024/.

Stop calling yourself small and start claiming the space your business deserves.

This chapter teaches you to stop operating like a "small business" and start managing your closely held company as an investable asset. Think like an investor: Define the future you're building toward, install the few systems that increase equity value, and measure progress the way public companies do. When you adopt this investor mindset from day one, including a clear exit plan, you make better decisions, move faster, and build transferable value that funds your financial independence.

Specifically, you will:

- Reframe your identity from owner-operator to owner-investor.
- Translate big-company rigor into lightweight, weekly systems you can actually run.
- Tie daily operations to equity value and a future exit, so every decision compounds.

Society calls them small businesses, but that label masks their true power. These so-called "small" companies, 99.9 percent of all US businesses with under five hundred employees, drive 44 percent of our GDP.[2] They're the ones creating jobs, launching daily, and sparking the innovation that transforms industries.

The label "small" is misleading. These are closely held businesses that are either on their way to greatness or already there, just not publicly traded. When we downplay their significance, we erode the entrepreneurial spirit that fuels innovation and transforms communities. We start thinking we should only invest in "large" things, missing the strategic opportunities right in front of us.

Your business size doesn't determine how you operate. You need a bigger

---

2   "Frequently Asked Questions About Small Business, 2024."

lens to see your full potential because there's nothing small about the families depending on you, the dreams you're supporting, the education goals you're funding, or the financial independence you're creating.

There is nothing small about those. That's why we business owners lose sleep, knowing we carry the aspirations not just of our own and our companies but also of every team member walking through our doors.

Adopting a Bigger Business Mindset

If you're not small, then you're big. You need a bigger business mindset. The methodologies that power public companies can be repackaged for closely held businesses, helping you get there faster.

When my clients kept asking how to structure businesses that would outlast them, I realized there are really no new business ideas—only better ways to apply proven strategies to the businesses that matter most.

Public companies already have systems that are required to be implemented on a daily, weekly, and monthly basis. Let's bring the helpful elements of what they're doing from Wall Street to Main Street. We can develop patterns that match what investable companies are doing and apply them to your closely held business.

Planning Your Exit from Day One

Every business owner will exit their business one way or another: through the exit door, through a fire sale, through a transition to employees or shareholders, or to an outside party. You have to prepare for that every step of the way, not just three years out, but seven to ten years out.

My favorite client experiences are the ones where we start a business together, and we're already talking about what the exit is going to look like from day one.

To do that, you must understand the value of your business, the key drivers, and the levers you can pull to realize the larger exit you eventually want. Then, you have to install systems that document that those levers are being pulled and that you're maximizing the value of the business.

For one client, we identified that we needed clear operational goals connecting the people, manufacturing, and financial results. We set up metrics for their operating team—all the items they needed to hit on a regular basis. For the owner, we equated that to the value movement of the company.

We helped determine a value for the company, created an actual stock price, and even gave them a ticker symbol.

The owner watched his per-share price grow to a point where he knew that if we sold at that final point—and we did—it would support his financial independence into the future.

Very few of our owners ever want to completely retire. They want to work forever, and that's cool. But financial independence gives them the opportunity to do whatever they want, whenever they want.

From Operator to Owner-Investor

A small business owner maybe looks at what they need to do for the day, but not the next 10, 30, or 150 days. We've heard the popular saying before: They're working *in* their business, not *on* it, doing what they need to survive.

We've all been there. You have to do some of the daily things, but you also have to keep your mind looking further out, forecasting and planning for the future, laying the groundwork and investing in the business.

Sometimes a small business is a lifestyle business that won't be transferable to another owner. That's fine because you can make a ton of money with it, and it can feel great for the business owner and the team. But that situation is all about them, their goodwill, and what they can generate. It's not worth much of anything to anyone else.

I have a great client—she's a lobbyist with a small team, and they're changing rural health care in our state. She gets paid handsomely, and she's doing the things she needs to do. But she can't sell that; it's about her, and that's okay. It's a lifestyle business. Some people have single licensed-distributor contracts or arrangements where they really can't build transferable value.

I've worked with business owners to explore multiple distribution contracts and find different ways to memorialize and transfer value to their families, even if not to an outside party. There are ways to build value, but some businesses remain inherently tied to the people running them.

The Strategic Reinvestment Decision

A business owner faces a critical choice: Take money out as wages or distributions, or reinvest strategically in areas that will grow future value. This decision requires purpose and a clear end game: building the equity value that ultimately funds your future independence.

Systems that unlock growth present an interesting challenge. When I tell most clients we should implement practices from publicly traded companies, they immediately think of waste and duplicity.

Large corporations don't exactly scream efficiency. But this doesn't mean we need to embrace the inefficiencies of massive corporations. Instead, we can adopt the scaling tools and processes that Fortune 500 companies use and apply them strategically to closely held businesses.

Bringing Wall Street Systems to Main Street

My career gave me a unique vantage point. I started at the world's largest CPA firm, working with publicly traded companies like State Street,

Colgate-Palmolive, and AMC Theatres. Inside these companies, I witnessed the critical importance they placed on structure, reporting, and forward-looking statements—even more than backward analysis. These tools aren't irrelevant for small businesses. When you're always looking in the past, business becomes chaotic and reactive, constantly comparing performance to prior years instead of measuring against what you intended to accomplish this year.

So without that structure of laying out what you're going to do, even the best ideas will not make it off the cutting room floor. So if we look at how the publicly traded companies are set up, we can use some of their systems.

But also know that we can speed up, we can pivot fast, and we can fix things that don't work for us in a faster, more meaningful way.

We don't have to impose bureaucracy to create systems, but we need to take on the mindset of larger companies. CEO Andy Jassy mentioned that for Amazon to survive, they needed to operate the world's largest start-up.[3] Size doesn't kill speed. Lack of clarity does.

Amazon wants to be you, the closely held business owner right there. They're a little jealous that you aren't having to turn an aircraft carrier every time you want to make a decision. Installing some of the systems that enable them to do that won't slow you down; they'll actually speed you up.

I also really enjoy reading about Sara Blakely and SPANX. Not because those things are comfortable, but because she bootstrapped and built the company from the second bedroom in her apartment, not taking any outside investment and reinvesting the profits in growing organically. She never gave up any control. She had a vision for the future of product development and what the value of this business could one day be. She never

---

3   Amazon Staff, "CEO Andy Jassy shares 7 ways Amazon strives to operate like 'the world's largest startup,'" Amazon News, April 14, 2025, https://www.aboutamazon.com/news/workplace/ceo-andy-jassy-amazon-worlds-largest-startup.

looked back and was unafraid to make investments in her business to get the valuation she wanted.[4]

Looking at adding systems, rigor, planning, and forecasting will push you forward, not hold you back.

Your Next Moves

- Identify your blockers. Name the top two: time scarcity, fear of complexity, lack of metrics, perfectionism, or "I'll do it later." Action: Choose one system to install this quarter (weekly scorecard, ninety-day plan, or monthly forecast).
- Shift identity from owner-operator to owner-investor. Write a one-sentence investor thesis for your company and list three to five value drivers you'll grow (e.g., gross margin, recurring revenue, customer concentration, retention).
- Define an exit horizon. Pick a seven-to-ten-year target, a valuation range, and likely buyer type (strategic, financial, internal). Back into three-year and one-year targets.
- Install a lightweight operating cadence: a weekly leadership meeting with a five-to-ten-metric scorecard, a monthly forward-looking forecast, quarterly priorities with owners and due dates.
- Tie operations to equity value. Create a simple "stock price" proxy using revenue quality, gross margin, churn/retention, NPS, and cash-conversion cycle. Review it monthly.
- Set a reinvestment rule. Reinvest a fixed percentage of free cash flow into value drivers before taking distributions.

---

4   Dave Smith, "Billionaire Sara Blakely says she launched Spanx with just $5,000 from selling fax machines—and never took on a single investor: 'I bet on myself,'" *Fortune*, msn.com, September 20, 2025, https://www.msn.com/en-us/money/ technology/billionaire-sara-blakely-says-she-launched-spanx-with-just-5-000- from-selling-fax-machines-and-never-took-on-a-single-investor-i-bet-on-myself/ ar-AA1MXo95.

Document how you'll deploy it each quarter.

- Derisk key-person dependency. Document your top five processes, cross-train, and de-risk your key person dependency .
- Fix pricing and mix. Audit pricing against value, kill low-margin work, and overinvest in your highest-lifetime-value customer segments.
- Build scalable demand. Test two to three repeatable acquisition channels with small bets; keep what compounds and cut what doesn't.
- Get capital ready. Clean your books, separate personal from business, close the month within ten days, and start a basic data room (contracts, KPIs, org chart, SOPs).
- Challenge limiting beliefs. Write down the belief that's keeping you "fine where you're at," then run one thirty-day experiment to disprove it (e.g., raise price 10 percent, delegate one role, ship one new offer).
- Pick your next move now. Choose one system to implement in thirty days, assign an owner, set a due date, and book the first review meeting.
- Resource: Read *The E-Myth* (Michael E. Gerber) to build systems and structure around your growth plan—not just operations.

We're no longer small business owners. We are investors in our corporation, and we need to start thinking like it.

As an investor in a corporation, we expect systems and plans for growth installed and working before we invest any money. You're giving yourself money every day. So why don't we move forward?

We're not going to use the terms *small* versus *big* any longer. We're just going to use the terms *public* versus *private*. We're going to start looking at how public companies do the things they need to survive and grow, to continue attracting investors and generating very large returns.

This isn't easy, but it is incredibly valuable.

CHAPTER 2

Steal the Systems That Power Billion-Dollar Growth

Public CEOs face investors every ninety days. Private owners rarely face that mirror. That's why value stalls.

Watching an earnings call on CNBC, I realized the questions public CEOs must answer—future, risks, strategy—are the questions most private owners never get asked. So we stole their system.

After explaining the concept over and over with no one really seeing the connection, I figured I'd appeal to my coworker Chris's favorite beverage. So I walked them through how Coca-Cola does it. The moment I said, "If it's good enough for Coca-Cola, it's good enough for us," everything clicked.

We needed public-company rigor without public-company bureaucracy. Today, we run quarterly "investor calls" inside our clients' private companies: one page, hard questions, clear commitments. If it's good enough for Coca-Cola, it's good enough for us.

This chapter shows you how to think like an investor, not an owner-employee, and install the discipline that builds real enterprise value.

Through this process, we'll dissect the disciplines and controls that public companies rely on and determine which ones apply to your business. That gives us clarity of direction, clarity of expectations, and clarity of value creation.

We'll then shift our focus from a foundation of clarity to returns and building a business that's truly investable, one that others would compete to own.

The end goal isn't just personal financial independence; it's creating generational stability for you, your family, and the people who help you build it.

Developing the Investor Mindset

Most business owners struggle to transition from working inside their business to operating as a true CEO who answers to investors. When you were the best salesperson your company ever had, it's natural to focus on what made you successful in that role. But you're the CEO; growing the value of your business isn't just about growing revenue anymore.

You need to develop an investor mindset. Take a five-thousand-foot view of your business with investor-level discipline. Without this perspective, you muddle through growth plans without connecting them to increased business value. You might earn a good salary and take distributions, but you're never truly working on building enterprise value.

Think how publicly traded companies operate. In their investor calls, CEOs articulate their vision for the future, and analysts use that information to determine the company's future value. You need to set the same kind of vision, one that establishes clear return expectations for how much you can grow your value and what that growth will look like.

During our quarterly planning meetings with our clients that mirror these investor calls, we ask pointed questions: "You said X. What does that mean for company value? You have labor issues in Kansas. How does that affect the rest of the company?" We examine risks, opportunities, and distributions, and what everything means for future value. When you start seeing your company through this lens and looking around corners, your confidence in decision-making soars, and so does your performance.

The Vulnerability of Transformation

The first time that business owners hold these meetings, they feel wildly vulnerable, like I'm attacking them. And I understand why. You didn't become a business owner because you thought you knew a little bit about your business; you're an expert. You've been doing this alone—maybe with a good management team, but still fundamentally alone.

These business owners have to become open to feedback and willing to examine things differently, trusting that this process will eventually produce results.

Some meetings are better than others, depending on the headspace people bring to these discussions. But when people see movement in the right direction over time and recognize how this approach helps identify blind spots, they become completely invested in the process.

At first, it will be awkward because you're doing something different. It's not that you weren't successful or don't know your business. You just don't know what you don't know.

We get trapped in our echo chambers, hearing only ourselves. Opening up to questions becomes a vulnerable but essential process.

Understanding the Choice to Stay the Same

Why do business owners struggle to shift from an operator mindset to an investor mindset? If what they were doing before worked fine, they often don't understand the risks of doing nothing or staying the same.

Some reach a place of complacency where what they're doing is enough; they don't want to work harder or invest more. That's okay. I've worked with many clients who go through this process and decide they'll sell in three years, keeping things as they are.

That works sometimes. During other times, though, something bad happens before then, and the family ends up selling the business.

Through our firm's acquisitions of CPA firms, I spend considerable time talking to owners about their visions for the future. Many are content making the same money and doing the same role day in and day out. Not everyone is positioned for growth, and that's fine, but you need to understand that you are making a choice by changing nothing.

My dad's closest friend sold life insurance, and many things that come out of my mouth are from him. He would say, "Buy the life insurance or don't—but don't pretend you didn't choose. Indecision is a decision."

The problem isn't choosing to be an operator versus an investor; it's behaving as an operator without realizing you want to be an investor, or not knowing what you're leaving on the table.

If you know what you've left behind, fine. Hiring eighty more CPAs and expanding into twenty more markets sounds exhausting. I can do the math to see if "exhausting" is worth it.

Borrowing Wall Street Rigor Without the Complexity

Let's borrow the best of public company standards. Public companies have layers of governance. Their structure, governance, planning, and rules drive their success, not hinder it.

For a company to be listed on a publicly traded exchange, the Securities and Exchange Commission requires annual and quarterly reports. As a grunt at the world's largest CPA firm, I had the privilege of personally adding up the numbers on these reports to ensure their accuracy before they went to investors.

These reports create systems of internal alignment for accurate historical reporting that people can trust. Looking to the past shows exactly what companies already did. Accurate historical financial statements matter, but so does the ability to forecast into the future with consistency.

You don't have to be on Wall Street to adopt Wall Street rigor. Most companies don't need quarterly CPA reviews, but we can embrace that thought process: systems where we measure what we're doing, review historical results quarterly, and align them with strategy for the next quarter.

Even if you're the only one asking yourself questions, this practice is valuable. The more people you can bring in to ask questions, however, the better.

Many business owners gauge performance by checking account balances daily or weekly. While cash availability and key numbers matter, examining financial results more deeply helps clients gain clarity about the numbers driving their business and improves decision-making.

This isn't about issuing a 120-page document like publicly traded companies. I'm talking about creating quarterly financial statements with operational metrics important to your business, all on one page. It doesn't require complexity, but it demands a commitment to financial reporting and periodic discussions that build confidence in the financial numbers you use for forecasting.

The Danger of Single-Metric Obsession

I see plenty of leaders latch onto a single number and assume it tells the whole story. The client who only watches cash is blind to everything else that drives the business.

Some focus solely on receivables or one line in their financials and assume that's enough. It never is.

One client illustrates this perfectly. Once we analyzed revenue per machine—how many machines they had, what each produced, and how that showed up quarter after quarter—it became obvious that their true metric wasn't cash in the bank. The meaningful insight was operational: the number of machines and the productivity of each. They could walk into the warehouse and see performance with their own eyes. The bank balance, on the other hand, didn't always reflect reality.

That's the value of shifting from a single view to a multilens perspective. You gain more ways to understand the same business.

Without measurement across multiple points, you drift. And when you drift, you either obsess over the wrong thing—or miss what matters altogether.

Holding Yourself to Public Company Standards

Hold yourself to a higher standard. Public company CEOs get fired all the time because shareholder returns are the scoreboards. As an owner, you are being fired by no one—but that doesn't mean the standard should be lower. The real question is: Did you do what you said you'd do?

Public CEOs openly discuss risk, shifting strategies, labor shortages, weather disruptions—whatever is affecting performance. They acknowledge uncertainty. We need to use the same level of honesty with ourselves. Ask the uncomfortable questions about the future: What stands in the way? What needs to change? What must I execute to get there?

Then hold yourself accountable.

Without that discipline, it's easy to slip back into operator mode—reacting rather than leading like an investor. Think of yourself as your own board or questioning committee. If needed, have technology push the hard questions.

Upload your financials metrics and what you committed to do last quarter into your trusted AI tool and enter the following prompt: "Act as an activist investor on an earnings call." Based on this data, ask tough questions about:

- variances vs. forecast
- margin compression
- customer concentration
- cash flow
- capital allocation
- risk exposure
- competitor

Better yet, build your own advisory circle. Surround yourself with people who challenge your assumptions, elevate your thinking, and push you toward long-term impact—for the business, for your personal wealth, and for true financial independence.

Facing the Fear of Your Own Earnings Call

Ask yourself: If I were on my own quarterly earnings call with outside investors in the business, what would I say? How would I respond?

That thought scares many founders. It causes uncertainty, which is what moves the stock market up and down every day. If we were certain of tariffs, tax positions, and the world economy, the market wouldn't move much. There would be no daily ups or downs.

Sometimes our clients who don't see their stock prices rolling across the bottom of a screen don't realize the actual amount of uncertainty they're facing. Their stock prices are going up and down every single day. They just don't have the ability to look at it on a ticker on CNBC.

When you start saying that the future value of your final exit and your actual financial independence is reliant upon how you face these uncertainties and how you invest in your business in the future, that's a scary proposition—because you're the one making the decisions. This is all on you.

Many founders aren't even sure what they would say. They aren't even sure exactly how well positioned their company is financially. They don't even know the questions to ask because they're so deep in the weeds.

I have privately held business owners who go to industry meetings, connect with their peers, and are always aware of what's going on in their industries. But do they apply this knowledge? Do they ask themselves where they fit? They need to be aware of the unique risks inside their businesses that they might be ignoring.

Key Takeaways

- Run a quarterly, one-page investor-style review: Set a vision, examine risks, and connect results to future value.
- Track multiple operational metrics (including machine productivity) instead of fixating on a single number like cash.
- Adopt public-company rigor without bureaucracy: Produce accurate quarterly financials, forecast results, and align strategy.
- Hold yourself to public-company standards: Ask uncomfortable questions, name uncertainties and roadblocks, and hold yourself accountable.
- Install accountability: Treat yourself like your own board or build an advisory circle to challenge assumptions.
- Embrace the vulnerability of the process: Openness to feedback reveals blind spots and improves performance over time.
- Face your "earnings call" fear: Answer tough questions about the future of the business and the uncertainty you're facing.
- Make a conscious choice: operator or investor? Understand and accept the trade-offs if you choose to stay the same.
- Treat your business as an asset that must deliver returns, not just a paycheck.

This simple step of committing to regular financial review meetings gives you clarity that leads to enjoyment. What if you could count on things? What if you could address uncertainty and dial it down just a little, knowing you can count on something that's working? That would be nice.

Now you're flying at five thousand feet. You are an investor in your business, and it's time to start demanding returns and results, just like you would if you owned shares in Coca-Cola. You need to treat your business as an asset that delivers returns, not just a paycheck—an asset that delivers results in various forms.

CHAPTER 3

Demand ROI Like an Investor

Most business owners obsess over their monthly income while completely ignoring whether their businesses are actually building wealth. They're trapped in a dangerous cycle: working inside their company instead of investing in its growth, being focused on what they can pull out today rather than what it could generate tomorrow.

The math is sobering. For 80 to 90 percent of business owners, their companies represent nearly their entire net worth.[1] Their dreams of financial independence hinge entirely on this single asset. Yet they treat it like a job that pays wages instead of an investment that should generate returns.

When that much of your net worth sits in a single private asset, your risk is higher than a hedge fund's worst day. Concentration isn't strategy; it's exposure.

Here's where it gets worse. Most take any excess cash and either stuff it in a bank account "just in case the business needs it" or invest in companies that look exactly like theirs. Contractors buy construction stocks. Restaurant owners invest in hospitality. They think familiarity equals safety, but they're actually doubling down on risk.

The illusion of control drives this behavior. Business owners believe they

---

1   Colleen Kowalski, "Understanding Exit Planning," Exit Planning Institute (blog), January 9, 2023, https://blog.exit-planning-institute.org/understanding-exit-planning-epi-and-maus-partnership.

can control their companies' fate, so they keep everything tied up in them. But they don't control market shifts, economic downturns, or the countless external forces that can devastate any industry overnight.

Would you put 90 percent of your investment portfolio into UPS stock just because the driver comes to your door every day and you decide whether to open it? Of course not. Yet business owners routinely put that much of their wealth into a single company they believe they control.

Then, they compound the problem. They buy the real estate their business operates in, purchase supporting companies in the same industry, and even hire family members. They're building what looks like a diversified empire, but it's actually a house of cards built on a fault line in the same economic neighborhood.

The cruelest irony? They think they're reducing risk when they're actually stacking it higher . . . like reinvesting dividends into the same stock for years, then wondering how they ended up so concentrated in one position.

Your business should pay you twice: once as income while you work in it, and again as returns on the risk you're taking by owning it.

Stop managing for wages. Start managing for ROI. Your business must pay you twice—wage now, equity later—and you will run it like an investor: Set a target return, track it, and reinvest systematically to increase enterprise value for the person taking the risk every day, the owner.

Business owners may build systems that provide nice wages for their efforts but no returns for the risk they're taking. They're seeing higher revenues and results, but they don't realize their actual equity and value in the business are flat. They're doing more work for fewer actual returns.

Thinking Like an Investor in Your Own Business

You must set systems in place to track returns and create value where your inputs don't constantly equal your efforts, where you can maintain a solid level of effort but see a disproportionate increase in returns.

One of my favorite clients owns satellite dish installation companies, the ones that go to your house and put the dish on your roof, then connect it to your TV. He was one of the first people who really taught me to look at business differently. We were working on his forecasts and financial statements when he said, "Just keep redoing it till I at least get 12 percent to the bottom line."

"Why 12 percent?" I asked.

"Why would I work this hard, take on all this risk, oversee all these people for anything less than a 12 percent return? Michele, I can take this bad boy, sell it, put it in the market, and let my investment advisor give me 12 percent."

The correlation isn't perfect, but I understood. What he was saying was, "If I'm not running this business to produce results, why am I working so hard? I'll just put it in the market, let the market work for me, and cash out." That client helped me see that you're not just the CEO; you're the largest investor in your business, and you need to start acting like it.

The Wealth-Building Machine vs. the High-Paying Job

The distinction between a high-paying job and a wealth-building machine is crucial. You might pay yourself $500,000 a year. Amazing, right? But if you're taking that money out to the detriment of your business's future value, then when you go to sell, you won't have anything to sell.

You can take all the earnings out to support your lifestyle and let the business languish. Instead, you might take $400,000 out and invest $100,000 back into your sales force or whatever will increase future value based on your projections. You need to invest in tomorrow's value, not just take the money out today.

When I look at the CPA firms we acquire, most are partnerships with three or four CPAs in the later stages of their careers. They're looking around, saying, "Do I stay here and keep this business so I can get two more years of $500,000 in salary, and then sell it? I'm not going to put in that newfangled electronic filing system. I'm going to keep everything in file cabinets. I'm not going to invest in the highest-grade technologies or try to attract new CPAs. I'm just going to take my profits and run."

Then we come into their firm and say, "Oh my gosh, you have great clients and good people. But I'm going to have to spend so much time and money investing in your filing system, IT system, and culture, because everybody knows you were just milking it right until the end. So instead of paying 1.5 times revenue, I'm going to pay 0.5, because I'm not buying your problems."

That's what other people will see when they look at you. If you just take all the money and don't reinvest it, you're pretaking your future exit price. You're taking it now, and you're not going to get it later. We don't know what multiple you're giving up, but you can take it now, or you can take it later.

The high-paying job can be nice if you're getting $500,000 a year. That's fantastic. But when it comes time to sell, you won't get much gold in the pot at the end of the rainbow. The alternative is treating this as a wealth-building machine. You're getting your wage, but then at the end, there's a multiplier—a completely different outcome.

If you can invest and grow your business and find a strategic buyer who sees the value you've created plus what they have, that multiple is one we don't know. You could be leaving so much money on the table by taking it all out now.

Return on Time: Making Every Hour Count

Endless effort isn't a strategy. Throwing everything at the wall and seeing what sticks doesn't necessarily add value; it's a stall. You don't know what's going to stick unless you spend the time to understand the key value drivers of your business and focus on those.

If I'm asking you to invest in your business, we'd better have a good investment case and proof that it would add to the fair market value of your company. We have to measure not only the returns from the business but also the inputs—where you spend your time and how they align with the strategic objectives that are the true drivers of value for your business.

If we've decided the most important thing is finding a strategic revenue stream—like developing a subscription model, better documenting contracts, or finding higher-performing vendors—then that's where your focus must be.

When you've identified the three or four strategic priorities that truly move the needle, everything else becomes a distraction. That business opportunity in another state or that additional service line aren't inherently bad ideas. But if pursuing them means abandoning your core focus, you're trading potential breakthrough results for scattered efforts.

This clarity gives you the power to say no—not just to external opportunities but also to the internal voices that whisper, *We could also do this.* You already have your answer: *We're spending our time here, and we're doing it this way.*

Success follows a pattern of behaviors that multiply and grow over time. As the CEO of your own life and business, you must align your calendar with these strategic priorities. If you were running a publicly traded company and failed to execute on your stated goals, you'd be fired. The same accountability applies to you.

This isn't about working harder; it's about working smarter and saying no to everything that isn't a strategic priority.

We call this *return on time.* If you invest five hundred hours in a strategic initiative and can forecast the results, you can measure that return. When your efforts generate a 15 percent increase and $2 million in value from five hundred hours and $500,000 invested, you've won. But you have to see the end game.

Private equity professionals excel at this. They build detailed projections showing how a prerevenue company with zero clients can be worth $20 million. It seems impossible. How does an idea with no customers equal $20 million in value? They see the market, understand the mechanics, and know that $5 million and three years of focused time can create that valuation. Those "pie in the sky" projections aren't fantasy; they're road maps built on strategic clarity.

We have real business owners who are doing these things every single day; we can use those same thought processes to see how they really impact valuation, but in a meaningful way to the business owner.

Doubling Enterprise Value Through Strategic Diversification

I worked with an electrical contractor whose focus was to add one new line of service to their existing business. Most of their current revenue was tied to projects for new multifamily construction. They assessed their current teams and connections and realized that they could provide belowground cable and electrical work as well. That was a different line of service with a new set of customers and contracts, but it was aligned with their primary focus. They had to invest in the equipment and train the operators for those machines, but it was not out of their line of expertise—it was still electrical work.

They originally had significant concentration risk by only serving large multifamily projects working within only a handful of general contractors. In a market like Chicago or Kansas City, the barrier to entry for that niche is low. Anyone with a solid reputation and a capable team could show up and replace them or underbid them.

Diversification changed everything. They expanded both their service offerings and their client base. Now, instead of relying on one narrow category, they have more than twenty active clients, including new work like underground electrical projects just down the street.

By adding a new service line and diversifying cash flow sources, they reduced dependence on any single segment. That shift to more offerings, more clients, and more revenue streams significantly increased their value. That was all because of a realignment from the founder's perspective.

Instead of spending time to find more multifamily-build opportunities or doubling down on the things that he had previously known, he found that his time was better served adding a different service. So instead of spending the five hundred hours on repeated actions, he spent the five hundred hours starting a new line of service.

Key Takeaways

- Identify the key value drivers in your business and let them guide where you spend your time.
- Check to see if you're focusing on the right things or simply repeating what you've always done.
- Don't just work in the business—implement your strategic plan so you don't leave growth on the table.
- Review recent initiatives to spot paths you shouldn't have gone down and what they crowded out.
- Be clear about what truly moves the needle and align your daily activities with that intention.
- See the direct line between how you manage your time and the impact on your business.
- Stop underestimating the value of your time.
- Learn from past wastes of time (flashy product lines, misfit partners, shiny employee ideas) and say no sooner.
- Remember the real cost of distraction: not just money and legal fees, but months of your life—sometimes as much as six months—that you can't get back.

We're going to "go public." The first step is to build an advisory board and surround ourselves with the kinds of leaders who will challenge us to grow—to help us set our strategic priorities and get the returns that we know we can.

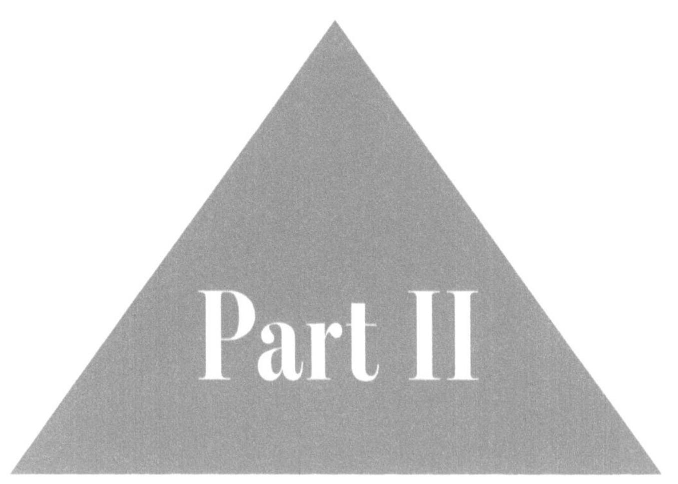

Install Public-Grade Systems

CHAPTER 4

Build an Advisory Board That Actually Moves the Needle

When I tell clients to build a board of advisors, they hear "Give yourself bosses," and their first reaction is predictable resistance. They didn't start their own business to answer to anybody else. But eventually, they realize that they can't build a business in a vacuum.

Using an advisory board can accelerate your business growth by surrounding you with people genuinely invested in your success.

I can imagine the skepticism: "You want me to give myself bosses?"

Exactly.

"I'm not here for accountability. I'm a cowboy running my business the way I want to do it."

But that isolation becomes your weakness. You know the saying "It's lonely at the top"? It's also an echo chamber where you're surrounded by people who tell you what they think you want to hear instead of what you *need* to hear.

An advisory board changes everything. Instead of bouncing ideas off just one person, like your friend or your spouse, you get multiple perspectives actively engaged in challenging your thinking and expanding your vision. Yes, they hold you accountable, but that's how you grow.

I can't hold myself accountable. If I say I'm only going to drink wine once a week, who am I arguing with when I break that promise? What real consequence exists?

You can sabotage yourself in countless aspects of your life and business this way. That extra ounce of accountability, partnership, and team support is what takes your business to the next level.

We've already discussed why advisory boards matter. The real conversation is about choosing the right people, understanding why they're the right fit, and then truly leveraging their expertise and time.

It's more than assembling smart individuals. The value comes from alignment: getting the right people focused, engaged, and rowing in the same direction to drive meaningful results for the business.

From Isolation to Insight

I have a board of directors for our CPA firm that functions as an insightful group challenging our limiting beliefs. They help me stick to our core beliefs as an organization and allow me to not just function based upon my narrow view of what I believe to be important. We have a group; it's not just one managing partner making all the decisions. We've started to thrive more and more as an organization when we switched to this corporate methodology of leveraging a board of directors.

If you have a managing partner, they only have their one skill set to push things forward as well. That's not enough.

Our board of directors allows us to move from solo decision-making to real traction because we're able to bring people along in the strategic plans faster. All the members of my board of directors work in the business. I'm recommending that business owners go outside of their business and build an independent advisory board.

Building Your Independent Advisory Board

That board isn't meant to oversee you. It is meant to enhance your limits as an individual. The members are there to bring enhancements to your decisions and to how you want to scale and where.

The strategic thing is that they're there to support you, not to hold you back. We're looking to find three or four trusted advisors you can bring together from outside your company, who bring different levels of experience and accountability. Then, we're going to formalize that group with timing, discussion points, agendas, and regularity.

This advisory board will allow you to throw ideas out there that aren't necessarily aimed at team members who might be impacted by the results of your discussions. The board brings an independent eye and view to the strategic plans and things that you want to do. It's not your spouse, who, when you ask if you should make a change that would impact your net income, says no because you plan to go to Europe in a few months. The board members have a vested interest in your success, but they're independent enough to provide you with that outside counsel and thought.

It takes a willingness to be vulnerable to find the right people, ask them to participate, and then put your ideas on the table, knowing they'll be examined, debated, or challenged.

One client who built an advisory board described the impact clearly. Preparing for the meetings, spending those two focused hours each quarter, and walking out either validated or constructively challenged gave him clarity and direction. He left each session with a future-focused plan and the confidence that others were in his corner.

Business ownership can be isolating. Even when we surround ourselves with peers, they're not always aligned with our success. In accounting, for example, many of us belong to associations or networks where we lean on one another—a kind of cooperative competition. We share ideas, but at the end of the day, we still want to win. That's useful, but it's not the same as having three or four trusted advisors committed solely to your growth.

That's why structure and selection matter. Not all advisory boards are equal. The right board must be built intentionally and aligned to your goals, business, and future.

There's often a defining moment in this journey. A founder once said, "I used to make every decision in a vacuum. Now I walk in with questions and walk out with direction." Most leaders realize that they never would've reached that level of clarity on their own.

I can speak directly to that transformation for many of my clients. They wouldn't have reached breakthrough moments alone. They wouldn't have thought in those expanded ways, and they feel more assured in their decisions because they know they have people there to support them.

The Power of Letting Ideas Breathe

Honestly, it's easier to surround myself with yes-men. But what comes out of that? Nothing good. It's the difference between knowing what is good *to* you and what's good *for* you.

I don't like to be pushed back on. I have a pretty strong personality. My gut reaction is to say, "I've already tried that" or "I've thought of that." But I have to be very purposeful when I throw a new idea out there to just let it breathe. Let it be dissected and made better. Every time I've opened my ideas and strategies up to improvement, they've always turned out better. I see that with my clients too. When they're working with their advisory boards, what they discover is that a strategy or idea isn't a *no*; it's just a *no, not right now*. Timing changes everything.

Our CEO, Brian, says that working with me is like working with a kid running around holding scissors. He never knows if I'm going to make a nice Mother's Day card or poke my eye out. That's actually a great characteristic for your chief strategy officer. You don't want someone who just keeps things the way they are. The best people to hold you accountable know what the safe boundaries for innovation are.

Rarely does my board tell me no, but I get a lot of "no, not right now." It's what you say to a kid. When I see my seven-year-old walking down the hallway with scissors, I don't say, "Stop." I check in: "What are you doing with those scissors? Can I give you some advice?"

Brian and I have been together twenty-one years. Not many partnerships last that long, but when you have the right structure and the right people, you feel empowered and supported.

What Separates Effective Boards from Social Hours

Here's what makes advisory boards work: The right people at the table can change everything. The wrong people waste everybody's time. If you're surrounding yourself with yes-men, it's not a board meeting; it's a party.

We've seen boards that were nothing more than social hours where advisors talk more about themselves than how their experiences can shape what the business owner is working on. These might be great people, but they're just not positioned to be good advisors right now.

It takes a special skill set to question without provoking, to guide without dragging someone along. It requires a relationship in which you feel comfortable being completely open and honest. If you have a group that's poorly structured or drains energy, it's just not fun, and you won't want to participate. But a great one expands your capabilities and the value of your company.

Finding the right people starts with personality assessments that reveal how they approach situations and their openness to real participation. Once you find them, structure becomes critical. We create a charter: *Here's what this board is responsible for, here's the time commitment, and here's what we're asking you to do. I promise to get everything to you in advance, and I'm not going to read slides to you in the meeting. We're going to talk. This is collaborative time.*

This isn't a dog and pony show. This is a brain trust. This board isn't your boss; it's the group you gather regularly to brainstorm and think about the future. You don't present to them. This is dialogue.

Pay people for these advisory roles because they're giving up their time to be invested in you. You show that investment by developing cadence, reporting structures, sticking to meeting schedules, keeping those meetings short and effective, and paying them for showing up.

I've been asked to join many advisory boards. When I show up and they hand me financial statements and complain about everything that happened in the last three months, the energy gets sucked from the room. That's not an advisory board—that's a book club. We're just getting together, having drinks, and bitching about life.

No questions get answered. No decisions on next steps get made. Instead, say, "During the last meeting, we talked about investigating something—did you? What do you think? What should we do?"

An advisory board isn't about looking backward at last quarter's revenue. It's about moving forward, and that forward momentum starts with one critical question: Who's in the room when you're running with scissors?

Here's what I plan to do this quarter. Did I do it? Should I not have done it? Should I add more? That's the conversation. Not a post-mortem—a playbook. We're talking about things in a safe way, with people who want you to keep running.

Setting Clear Expectations to Avoid Festivus

Before a person signs up to be your advisor, you need to set clear goals and expectations for that relationship and then make sure you do your part.

The hardest part is committing the time to set it up properly and sticking to the rhythm. That consistency is where most leaders fall off.

We help clients establish formal charters and recurring agendas for their advisory meetings. Advisors even sign an agreement outlining expectations, confidentiality, and participation standards. It removes the anxiety of sharing openly and ensures that everyone understands their role.

This isn't about inviting a friendly voice with no relevant expertise or an attorney waiting to bill by the hour. Advisory members should be independent, invested in the mission, and aligned with the purpose of the group. If someone isn't contributing, replace them. This isn't tenure; it's stewardship.

Advisory needs change as the business evolves. Coaches, mentors, and advisors serve best when there's clarity around expectations, timelines, and structure. Many advisors appreciate that clarity as much as the business owner does. When the framework is clear, they can show up with their best thinking.

If there's no structure and no intentional approach, the effort won't serve you. It can quickly devolve into a *Seinfeld*-style Festivus: lots of opinions, the airing of grievances, and not much progress. You may eventually get somewhere, but the path won't be efficient.

Start with alignment and purpose. Do the work you set out to do first. The feedback, the challenges, and even the grievances can come afterward.

The real power is in building an external advisory network that helps you think better, lead smarter, and grow stronger.

Learning from PepsiCo's Five C's Framework

Many CEOs believe no advisor could understand their business better than they do. But leaders like Indra Nooyi at PepsiCo prove the opposite. She not only built a formal external board, required for a publicly traded company, but she also carefully curated it using a clear framework. She prioritized what she called the five *C*'s: advisors had to be highly *competent*; had to be guided by a strong moral and ethical *compass*; had to have the *courage* to speak up; had to be willing to *communicate* openly; and had to be *consistent* in how they showed up.[1]

We all know brilliant people who stay quiet out of fear. Indra intentionally removed that barrier. Every time she engaged with her advisory group, her strategy sharpened. The business improved because the ideas were tested, not protected. Yes, managing independent advisors takes effort. Yes, it can be exhausting. But when done well, the return on that investment is undeniable.

Eventually, she expanded the model internally. Alongside her external board, she assembled an internal advisory group—people she could ideate with differently, people embedded in the day-to-day business. The structure stayed the same, but the conversations shifted based on context and responsibility.

Internal teams bring deep operational knowledge that outsiders simply can't replicate. External advisors bring perspective, objectivity, and industry breadth. Together, the balance creates stronger decisions.

Internal voices can also carry biases, and not every discussion belongs in front of the full team. But involving key leaders in structured, strategic dialogue develops them. It builds future executives and potentially future owners.

By modeling the discipline of advisory leadership now, you aren't just strengthening your strategy. You're also shaping the next generation of leadership that will carry the business forward long after you're out of the operator's seat.

---

1   PepsiCo, "Five C's of Leadership with Indra Nooyi," YouTube.com, August 26, 2011, https://www.youtube.com/watch?v=uoDMaydBOxk.

Key Takeaways

- Look for the people who already make you a little uncomfortable, the ones pushing you to grow, and invite them into a small, independent advisory network to strengthen your strategy and valuation.

- Start with your informal network, then identify gaps where you need specific expertise (finance, go-to-market, operations) to round out the board.

- Formalize the group: Set a simple charter and cadence and give advisors real space to challenge you under a clear methodology that leads to results.

- Audit your circle for echo chambers. If you keep hearing what you want to hear, add contrarians who will test your assumptions.

- Remember: This isn't losing control. Being the boss means choosing who gets to "boss" your ideas so that the best ones win.

- Engage advisors intentionally and consistently. Invite challenge, listen fully, and convert debate into decisions that move the business forward.

Start thinking about the people who already get under your skin with advice. The ones you know are right but whom, in the moment, you resist. An hour or a day later, you realize they were probably right.

I have a senior manager in our office, Chris. I know if I'm bringing an idea to him, it's about to be picked apart. He's a contrarian by nature. Even when I say he's a contrarian, he'll say, "No, I'm not." Then I'll say, "And that means you're a contrarian." He goes, "Yeah, I understand that. That means I'm a contrarian when I just told you I wasn't."

We'll be in a meeting, and I'll see him with a thought on something said. He wants to say it but doesn't know if this is the pick-apart time or not. He will literally take his finger, close his upper lip, and hold his mouth shut. I'll say, "Chris, do you have something you wanted to say?" "No." "Well then, you probably shouldn't have done your tell."

He will challenge and ask great questions. Then he'll say, "Okay, did that help at all?" "Yes, actually yes. Thank you." Finding those people and harnessing them—you're lucky if you can do that.

He's actually considering: *When do I share this? How do I share this? Is this the venue?* That's when I know I need him more. If I think I don't need help, it's probably the time I need the most help.

Next, we'll look at turning accountability into traction with metrics your team can act on daily. We'll choose three forward-looking operational indicators, build a simple scorecard and forecast, and adopt an "internal investor" rhythm so that advisory board conversations translate into measurable performance.

CHAPTER 5

Use Metrics to Drive Your Team's Performance

If your team waits forty days to learn what happened in the month before, you're flying blind and paying for mistakes you could have prevented yesterday. The fix is simple: Run your business on the few daily metrics that predict your financials.

We helped a business owner distill the actual key metrics driving their business and discuss them on a weekly and daily basis, rather than waiting for their financial statements. We found meaningful numbers that helped them understand their operations and predict the financial results they were going to have.

Instead of looking at the business based solely on what their profit and loss statement said, we started examining operational activities they could see happening every single day.

They could talk to their team about what they were doing physically each day and explain how those behaviors added up to the financial statements they would see in a few weeks or months. This helped them dial down to things that moved their business operationally and see the alignment of how that helped them financially as well.

The key is coming up with metrics that not just you as the owner know, but insights you can share with your team so they can see, when they improve processes how it impacts the day and the financial results for your business.

For a business driven by the number of hours their production line runs, managers can say, "We planned for eight hours today for our production line. We've decided that each hour it's open, we can make $10,000. So our goal today is to push for eight and a half hours to generate a little more revenue." That's on the revenue side.

More important are the cost considerations. *What is my operational cost for running that machine for that extra half hour? What does this really look like?* You're not waiting for some fancy profit and loss or cash flow statement, but saying operationally, *What are those actions I can take to help move the needle, and how do I talk about them in a meaningful way?*

It's easy to get intimidated by huge sets of financial statements. There's so much information that isn't helpful or useful. You must find a way to make authentic indicators that everyone can understand and act upon immediately.

Public companies do this all the time. They have to distill down the things that are important, the actual key value drivers for their business. They can't just look at it in the rearview mirror.

Look at it on a go-forward metrics basis and communicate that to the whole team so that you're all watching the same things—because keeping those things secret does nobody any good.

You might be shocked at what some of the largest private businesses are actually using to run their operations. Part-time servers at Applebee's have more real-time information about what's happening around them and what's available for selling than most business owners do.

The Timeliness Trap

The issue isn't just missing information; it's timing. Too many business owners don't see results until the prior month is closed. You might make a decision on July 1, but if you review financials quarterly and it takes twenty days to close, you may not fully understand the impact until late

October. Even a monthly close with a twenty-day delay leaves you steering the business through the rearview mirror.

You need forward-looking metrics (leading indicators), not just financial statements. Your financials should confirm what you already know from daily operations. For example, when we track machine hours, production volume, or asset utilization, we can predict outcomes before the financials arrive. I have a client in the coin-laundry space who knows revenue in real time just by monitoring how many machines are running and for how long. When the financials come in, we simply reconcile, not discover.

That level of visibility creates momentum. It allows you to adjust before mistakes become expensive. If you know what revenue is coming, you can actively manage expenses. Whether it's staffing a restaurant or a nursing home, when you understand the operational inputs driving revenue, you can make real-time decisions that create impact faster, without waiting months to find out what went wrong.

Predicting the Unpredictable

I used to work with restaurants at which certain days of the week were predictably slow, so they would staff accordingly. Then one day, they'd get hit and were understaffed. It felt unpredictable, but it really wasn't. "Oh well, this is the night of the annual festival, and we get hit every year. We could have known that."

It's not just that Tuesdays are slow. Different events and unique circumstances show up all the time. You have to be ready. Map and calendar out all the events happening because you could have a game or community event that night that might impact the whole area.

Sometimes your expectations don't align. Every once in a while, a bus gets dropped off in front of your restaurant, and you have to feed them. But that doesn't mean you overstaff next Tuesday just in case that bus shows up again.

Operations is a game of probabilities. While you want to be ready for the peaks, you would never make money by overpreparing. But knowing your key operational data—the things happening in the business that you can control—changes everything.

You can't control how many people come in the door, but you can control how many tables are set. If you're counting on 80 percent of the tables full, with a three-turn night, this is the staffing you need. At the end of every night, you can measure against what you did and start predicting what your results are going to be in the future.

The Forecast Revolution

The goal is developing forward-looking indicators, not just historical hindsight.

Most business owners fall into a deadly trap: They compare this month's income statement to last year's results, then spend their energy making excuses about different circumstances instead of taking control. They're constantly explaining why this year doesn't match last year, rather than measuring against what they said they would accomplish.

Create forecasts that lay out what you expect to happen, then compare your results to what you forecasted. Now you're not making excuses about external factors. You're either hitting what you committed to do, or you're not. I used to call it a budget, but that makes people uncomfortable. Nobody wants a budget. It feels like going on a diet. People think about budgets as limits on what they can spend, so think of it as a forecast.

A forecast is something you can modify, grow, and think through. Circumstances change during the year. Strategic priorities shift. You might discover that gross profit percentage matters more in your industry and find new ways to improve it.

Create your forecast, compare it to actual results, and tie it to operational data, and you become unstoppable.

The Three-Metric Scorecard

Most leaders don't need ten pages of data. They won't read it, and it won't drive action. Distill everything into three metrics that must move your business this month. Quite simply, I call this the Three-Metric Scorecard.

Take a coin-operated laundry model:

- Ninety-five percent of machines running with a thirty-minute repair time
- Average collection per machine of $1,500
- Capital expenditures: Spend less than 5 percent of revenue

Notice what's not listed: revenue targets or net income. Those operational metrics give everyone—collectors, repair techs, accounting—something specific and actionable. No one needs to wait for financial statements, and no one feels intimidated by the scorecard.

Scorecards lose value when the numbers are too big. Show someone $2 million and they'll freeze—they won't know where to start. Break it into three targeted actions, and the path forward is clear. When the scorecard is updated in real time—not forty days after month end—it becomes a tool for predictability and daily alignment.

This is the difference between being abstract and concrete. Don't talk about "reducing expenses." Talk about keeping repair time to under thirty minutes. We already know that time reduction saves $17 an hour, which drives major margin improvement. When the team hits that target, celebrate it. They don't need to know it saved $100,000. They just need to know they achieved the goal.

Large numbers mean nothing to most people. Actionable targets mean everything.

If I call our Kansas City repair team and say, "You overspent by $30,000 last month," the response is confusion: *Was it labor? Parts? Supplies?* But if I say, "Cut repair time to under thirty minutes," they know exactly what to do.

Closing a $2 million gap happens the same way: one focused action at a time. Take small bites of the whale—don't eat the whole thing at once.

Building Your Internal Investor Call

Public companies understand a beautiful rhythm to their operational communication. Every quarter, they must explain past results and where they're headed next. They discuss failures or outcomes that didn't match expectations, but they do it in language the Street understands so that investors buying their stock daily know the direction.

You need this same operational clarity when talking to your internal team, your advisory board, and future buyers of your business. When you can explain your past results and future direction tied to operational methodologies, you make your company more valuable.

Quarterly reviews don't work for every company. There are different business cycles and varying investments of time you want to make. You must pick what works for you. I have clients who meet three times yearly because quarterly feels like too much, and their business cycle keeps them busy nine months out of twelve. We build a plan that works with your schedule.

The publicly traded companies may report quarterly, but they're doing this work every month and every week. Find the right rhythm that transforms your business from excuse-making to unstoppable execution.

We've helped many clients build scorecards and reporting systems that create real accountability, tracking forecast versus actual and using those insights to drive strategic conversations. This mirrors how public companies operate. We even help clients structure agendas like investor calls, complete with the kinds of questions analysts would ask. Whether you review quarterly or every six months, the principle holds: What gets measured gets done. Also, you're not just measuring—you're leading with intention.

These sessions can feel uncomfortable. People ask what's missing, what you overlooked, and where the risks are. That pressure forces deeper thinking. Even preparing for an internal investor-style review can be eye-opening—the discussion becomes sharper, more thoughtful, and more productive.

Our strongest clients enjoy the challenge moments. They'll say, "I'm already ahead of you; we handled that. What else?" On real investor calls, a gotcha question signals trouble. In this environment, a gotcha moment signals growth: *I hadn't thought of that; great insight.* It's not negative; it's transformational.

In a public company, being caught unprepared can be damaging. Here, the response is simple: *Great question. What should I do with that?*

The most successful leaders look forward to these sessions. They're not seeking approval. They want interaction, challenge, and meaningful engagement—because that's where the breakthroughs happen.

Learning from Toyota's Playbook

Consider Toyota's approach to using metrics to drive their operations. Full disclosure: My family drives Toyotas, but we do have a Honda CR-V that's lasted through my sister-in-law and now my daughter.

Toyota invests in systems committed to a culture of continuous improvement. They can only know what to improve because they relentlessly report on what's happening. They have more metrics than any privately held company—not a one-page dashboard but extensive data with different people monitoring different aspects. These metrics, discussed daily and weekly, allow them to predictably forecast future performance and vehicle reliability.[1]

This is the difference between hoping for results and engineering them.

If you're not improving every day or every week, and you're waiting to the end of the year, you're falling behind. You can't be waiting to make a change for months on end. You need to know what's happening so you can course correct on a regular basis, and be disciplined in reporting and looking at and talking about the problems. I know it feels like a lot.

It even feels like a lot for Toyota. They track hundreds of metrics across their global operations. We're going to have three because we don't need to take on the bureaucracy of these publicly traded corporations. But we can incorporate the commitment, accountability, and the forecasting into our reporting and that culture of continuous improvement—what Toyota calls Kaizen.

Kaizen, which literally means "change for better" in Japanese, is the philosophy of making small, incremental improvements consistently over time. Rather than waiting for major overhauls or dramatic changes, Kaizen focuses on continuous, bite-sized enhancements that everyone in the organization participates in. It's the mindset that getting 1 percent better each week compounds into transformational change over the year. This is what I love about it—it's not about perfection tomorrow; it's about progress today. It's a mindset where you're committing to act, plan, check, and do on a large scale, and you're going to see the transformation.

The changes we're talking about are relatively small. We're not tracking everything or building a full department just to push out metrics.

With the technology you already have and a simple understanding of daily operations, you can pull a few meaningful metrics that drive visibility,

---

1   Jeffrey K. Liker, *The Toyota Way: 14 Management Principles from the World's Greatest Manufacturer* (McGraw Hill, 2004).

conversation, and forward forecasting. These allow you to make incremental improvements and spot deviations early, so course corrections are small, not dramatic. Toyota perfected this mindset, and while you don't need that level of complexity, you can distill the principles to fit your business.

The goal isn't to overreact every time something goes wrong or chase every fluctuation. Poor decisions come from reacting without good data. At the same time, we don't ignore patterns or explain them away as "one-offs." When something trends in the wrong direction, treat it like a yellow flag. It's not a crisis, just a signal to investigate.

Getting good at this takes time. Finding the right metrics that truly align with what matters requires iteration. But once the right indicators are in place, you gain a clearer picture of what's happening now and where the business is headed. That's when meaningful change begins.

Key Takeaways

- Identify the most critical operational metrics your team can improve to move the bottom line.
- Gather perspectives across layers (owner, frontline, advisory board) to craft metrics that are meaningful and actionable.
- Communicate these metrics regularly so that everyone understands how daily actions affect outcomes.
- Focus on weekly visibility of the key metric(s) and use it to course correct, not to blame.
- When results deviate, ask: What should we do differently next week? Or is this truly a one-off?
- Make performance data relatable for every stakeholder; clarity and relevance drive engagement and execution.
- Resource: *The Prosperity Playbook*, by Mackey McNeill—guidance on keeping metrics simple, aligned with operations and financials, and top of mind.

Now we have reporting rhythms in place. We know what we're doing. We know what we're looking at. It's time to stop repeating those mistakes so we can keep improving all those metrics. One of the most amazing ways to do that is to run some helpful postmortems and look at things not as failures, but as opportunities to improve.

CHAPTER 6

Conduct Postmortems Like a Pro and Stop Repeating Mistakes

If you really want to kick off a good meeting, start with "What did we do wrong?"

I didn't always create an environment where I enjoyed hashing through the things that went wrong. My nature is to focus on the positive. When I started asking my team, "What could we have done better?" it was pretty quiet.

What is she looking for here? Is it really safe to give these ideas? How do we share things without dishing out blame?

At first, I figured I would try it and see how it worked out. I quickly realized that if we didn't start creating a culture of assessing—not just celebrating our successes but also learning from the times that things could have gone better—we weren't going to be able to get to the next level.

Focus on turning setbacks into opportunities and on creating a culture where we can openly discuss what didn't work and use it to improve. Public companies do this routinely. On earnings calls, they're required to explain what went wrong, why it happened, what they're doing to fix it, and where they're headed next. That level of transparency is a powerful discipline private companies can adopt.

You don't have to do it publicly. You can do it behind closed doors with your team. The goal isn't to defend mistakes; it's to learn from them and decide how to move forward. When the culture supports honest postmortems and future-focused problem-solving, failure becomes fuel. That mindset, reflection with intention, helps take a business to its next level.

Facing failure, I avoided looking back because accountability assessments can feel personal and punitive. When people feel singled out, they stop taking risks. But you can reframe this culture entirely.

Reframing the Conversation Around Failure

Public companies report failures and misses every quarter. They just call them something different, from "extraordinary one-time items" to "softness in the segments." I don't even like the term *postmortem*—the concept of death doesn't inspire learning. Instead, ask, "What can we learn? What's our learning lab revealing? What did we say we'd accomplish this quarter that we didn't? What distracted us? What do we need to stop, start, or continue?"

Avoiding reflection means you're bound to repeat the same mistakes. How will you hit those ambitious targets doing the same thing repeatedly, expecting different results?

One thing we debrief constantly is whether we won or lost a client. We invest enormous energy in proposals and presentations. Believe it or not, sometimes we're not picked. Shocking, I know.

I take it personally every single time. That's probably why I had to create this whole culture around learning from failure. I'd find someone to blame—not verbally, not necessarily even my team, but some external force beyond my control. "The CEO's brother once worked at that other accounting firm. We never had a chance." "The market shifted. Who could've predicted it?" "Circumstances conspired against us." Externally, everything was working against us, so internally, none of it could be my fault.

But here's what I discovered: We can't only have these sessions when things go wrong. The meeting after the meeting already happens. People discuss what went wrong in pockets, away from leadership. Everyone on the factory floor already knows what needs to change. It just hasn't reached you yet.

From Reactive to Proactive Learning

When we put rigor around our quarterly learning labs for sales, we examined entire cycles: every touchpoint, every process improvement opportunity. The breakthrough came when people started applying lessons before they needed a postmortem. They'd prepare proposals already knowing what they'd learned from the last round.

The blameless "Stop, start, continue" format acknowledges reality: We need to start something new, stop wasting energy on what isn't working, and continue what's driving results. Not everything is bad; not everything is good. There's learning in every piece.

A well-run debrief doesn't just drive growth afterward; it also creates the culture and space to address problems while you're still working on the project. It's a pre-postmortem: *Regardless of whether I win this client, have I addressed everything that went wrong in the past?*

The companies that master blameless debriefs don't just survive their failures; they transform them into their competitive advantage.

Etsy does this: They conduct live debriefs almost in group-chat format. They pick apart projects, discuss the good and bad, and commit to do better next time. It's woven into their culture.[1]

But you can't just start doing that. You can't hop into Microsoft Teams

---

1   John Allspaw, Morgan Evans, and Daniel Schauenberg, "Debriefing Facilitation Guide" (PDF), extfiles.etsy.com, 2016, accessed February 1, 2026, https://extfiles. etsy.com/DebriefingFacilitationGuide.pdf.

and immediately start dissecting what might go wrong. You need to set the framework first, then focus on systems for the postmortem.

This means establishing how you talk about everything, regardless of project type, and ensuring you focus on improvement rather than scapegoating or blame. The right people need to be in the room with the right tone to run an effective debrief.

When we do this internally as a firm, we've uncovered hidden biases in how we present to clients. While we thought clients needed all thirty-five pages detailing how we'd take care of them, they needed something much simpler. They weren't getting what they needed from us.

Ask third parties—even clients who didn't choose you—what you could do better and bring that into your learning lab postmortems. Yes, it's vulnerable to ask a client why you weren't selected. But if you're truly curious and willing to course correct, ask the question. If you won't act on the information, don't ask.

You can run powerful debriefs and uncover hidden issues. Then it becomes cultural: a part of who you are and what you do every day, not something you wait for a meeting to address.

Building the Foundation

Culture needs time to develop. Setting intention before you begin questioning is incredibly important.

Your culture won't change overnight, and in the beginning, people may not believe you, especially if you had a culture of gotchas. When you ask everybody what went wrong, they'll assume that the gotcha is coming and that they'll be held personally accountable.

You have to flex that muscle and not allow that to happen through regular discourse. Do this over and over until people trust the process. That allows them to be free to explain, analyze, and give honest, blameless feedback.

Set aside the time and space, then give people the tools. If your culture would make people afraid of losing their jobs during postmortems, you probably need extra groundwork—maybe a book club reading a work by Brené Brown—to lay the foundation of where you're headed. Make it clear that you're not looking around to see who shouldn't be here anymore. You're looking for self-improvement.

Creating that culture of continuous self-improvement builds toward the end goal of progress.

When Solutions Stay Hidden

When issues stay hidden, performance plateaus. But there's a corollary: When solutions stay hidden, performance also plateaus. You might have found a solution, but if you don't communicate it, you're harming others.

That's the worst-case scenario: You knew what to do but weren't sharing it. This happens in organizations constantly.

Communication gets hard once you have more than two people. Knowledge sharing gets difficult. When you find a solution, instead of putting it on your "list for later," find ways to communicate it immediately.

Having a periodic process where you discuss what to stop, start, and continue creates space for sharing: "By the way, I came up with this thing. I already solved this last week." The response shouldn't be "Why didn't you share?" followed by "Well, the meeting was this week."

Yes, there are lots of meetings. But when you have a clear half hour set aside for process improvement with a clear agenda and safe space, you can get it done efficiently. These meetings don't have to take two hours. The first couple might, but once you get good at it, you move fast.

It's a "Slow down to speed up" approach. This could be slow at first, but once everyone has the rhythm and buy-in, the momentum builds.

Uncovering What Holds You Back

I don't help clients run postmortems. I give them the framework. Nobody wants the accountant in the room for postmortems. The person who tells the boss how much money they made or didn't make usually isn't the right person for this conversation.

Most of our internal postmortems focus on our sales process. One key discovery was when our presenters needed to give proposals so clients could actually see themselves in the solution, rather than our team presenting as CPAs with technical solutions.

Clients generally know what tax returns, financial statements, and audits are, but they don't know why they need them or what they mean for them. What peace of mind are they getting? We know the answer, but the client doesn't even know what questions to ask us to get that peace of mind.

We need to educate clients on how what we're proposing will provide peace of mind, forward-looking solutions that help them sleep at night. We know this comes through tax planning, forecasting, and business valuations. But those things are lame outcomes, not feelings. When you lead with the names of solutions, clients don't know what that means for them.

We discovered this through asking our clients, looking at what we'd been handing out, and realizing it meant nothing to them.

People don't really want to know what you're going to do for them. They want to know how you're going to make them feel and what problem of theirs you're going to solve. When I was telling clients they needed a forecast, I was essentially telling them they needed a budget—that they needed to go on a diet. Then I was trying to sell them a forecast.

My client's problem was that they needed significant bank financing to grow to the level they wanted. Guess what? That takes a forecast. That's what the bank needs to get comfortable. The client just knows he needs financing. If our proposal lists "Forecasts $10,000," they're thinking, *What's that?* But if we list "Assistance with a lending relationship $10,000"? Sold.

Speak their language.

That's what we learned through that process. You have to ask the questions, be willing to listen, and be open to do something different.

Our COO, Erika, always says you can ask questions of your team and clients, but if you don't plan on internalizing and acting on at least 80 percent of what you hear, don't ask. What a waste to survey employees once again just to tell them that you don't give a damn about what they're thinking.

Sometimes it's painful to hear that you suck or what you could do better. It rarely feels good. But if you're a vacuum cleaner and someone tells you that you suck . . . boom! You're winning.

Progress requires pain. It's not easy to reflect. You might hear things you didn't want to hear. But without those data points, how else will you grow? Ray Dalio's approach as outlined in his book *Principles* works because he's okay sitting in discomfort. He writes. "Pain + Reflection = Progress."[2] That's a muscle that must be built into your team to really get good, strategic information out of postmortems.

Sometimes it's hard to have the hard conversations. But once you establish psychological safety, pain and hard conversations become reflections. You might be looking back at something that didn't work out the way you wanted, but you operationalize the processes, and that leads to progress.

The key is not just doing this when something goes wrong. When it's something you simply do, it's not painful anymore. It's just part of how you operate.

---

2   Ray Dalio, *Principles: Life and Work* (Avid Reader Press/Simon & Schuster, 2017).

Making Reflection Routine

Reflection shouldn't be a hunt for mistakes; it should be part of how the business operates. Each quarter, we look at results, compare them to what we committed to, and ask three questions:

1.   What happened?
2.   How did it align with our plan?
3.   What can we improve next time?

Sometimes the answer is: *We did great; let's celebrate!* Reflection should happen in the wins, not just the hard moments.

Take the example where you realized clients weren't fully understanding what you offered. Yes, that realization stung, but the solution was simple: Change the language. No massive restructuring. No new software. No shutting down service lines. Just better communication, better framing, better words.

Words matter. They shape perception. They determine whether a client becomes a believer or walks away confused. In financial services, especially, knowledge means nothing if it can't be communicated clearly.

And that's just one example of the value reflection creates.

Sometimes insights lead to easy fixes, like discovering that a dashboard existed all along and simply needed to be shared. At other times, insights are more complex. The point is: You don't know what you don't know until everyone sits down together.

Reflection also brings clarity to choices, like whether late financial reports are truly a problem. Maybe the delay is fine and doesn't justify hiring. Or maybe it's worth investing in more capacity. Reflection gives you the space to decide whether to fix something or accept it.

Not everything needs a solution, but everything deserves a moment of

honest evaluation. That rhythm is where growth, clarity, and better decision-making take root.

Key Takeaways

- Use a blameless stop–start–continue to guide the conversation and keep it actionable.
- Mine mistakes on purpose. Surface them early and treat
  each one as data, not drama.
- Celebrate wins and standardize them so that success
  becomes repeatable across the organization.
- Share solutions immediately (don't wait for the next meet-
  ing); make learning visible team-wide.
- Set psychological safety rules: no names, no blame, a focus
  on processes and facts.
- Model vulnerability as the leader: Ask for feedback, thank
  people for candor, and avoid defensiveness.
- Assign owners and due dates for every agreed-upon action;
  review progress at the start of the next debrief.
- Level up your culture: read and discuss Amy Edmondson's
  The Fearless Organization as a team.

There's a founder I saw on YouTube who hands out one card per year to
each of his team when they start working for him. It's called the "I fu*ked
up" card.

If you still have your card at year's end, it means you weren't trying things,
weren't pushing boundaries. He's creating a culture of continuous improvement where not making mistakes means you weren't challenging yourself.

We can all stay in our lane and avoid risks, finding success to a certain
extent in a certain place. But real growth demands that we push beyond
that comfort zone.

You stop letting failure repeat itself. You get off the hamster wheel of repeating yourself over and over and over again, and critically think about the things you're doing in your business through building a culture of innovation and accountability. And that's going to drive value. So now it's time to get really clear on what drives your business value and how you can increase it. We'll uncover all those levers and really help shape what your business is and increase its value.

CHAPTER 7

Know Your Business's True Value and How to Increase It

Public markets don't buy your past. They invest in your future. Buyers pay for credible, repeatable, defensible cash flows. They invest in what your company will do next.

Shift from being an owner to a buyer. Owners chase revenue; buyers reward durable value.

We'll surface the hidden drivers beyond machinery, headcount, and basic processes and put them to work with two tools you can use this quarter: a Value-Driver Scorecard and a Forecast-to-Action Loop. You don't have to sell, but you should build a business the market would pay a premium for. This chapter shows you how to build that future on purpose.

What the Market Really Buys

Public companies aren't valued solely on what they've already accomplished; they're valued on what the market believes they'll do next. Their worth reflects the strength of the balance sheet, projected growth, talent investment, competitive position, and long-term strategy, not just today's revenue. These same value drivers are what private owners must consider when deciding where to improve. Without understanding how value is perceived, you risk investing time and money in the wrong areas—and eventually hitting a ceiling.

Even as a private owner, you must think like a public-company CEO whose performance is tied to stock price. That price reflects confidence in future results: credible forecasts, consistent execution, and a clear plan for growth. When you build reliable projections and follow through on them, you signal competence, discipline, and value creation.

That's what makes people want to invest in you or your business. And ultimately, that's what makes the company far more attractive and sellable.

The Power of Strategic Forecasting

You have to get good at forecasting, and those forecasts must align with strategic improvements. Buying equipment isn't valuable just because it adds an asset to the balance sheet. The value lies in what that investment enables.

One manufacturing client proved this out. By modeling the impact of new equipment and better training, we showed that a $1 million investment would improve gross margin by two percentage points. That margin increase alone would pay for the equipment in five years—and every year after that would generate additional profit. With that clarity, the decision became far less risky and far more strategic.

In that industry, buyers don't care how many widgets you sell—they care about gross margin. You could sell a million units at a 2 percent margin, and no one wants the business. But if you improve operational efficiency and boost margins, the company becomes desirable. Not only does the investment pay off the related debt, but it also increases the company's valuation and makes it easier to sell.

Had the owner simply repeated last year's behavior and avoided investing in margin improvements, he would have left more than a million dollars on the table at exit. Higher margins mean stronger multiples because the business performs better than the competitor down the street.

Forecasting gives you confidence. You're not guessing or hoping that a million-dollar purchase works out because you've already seen the projected return and the pathway to value. After a few cycles of doing this—forecasting, investing, measuring, and improving—you build muscle memory. You learn how to predict outcomes and deliver on them.

Buyers and investors reward that discipline. They avoid companies with unpredictable results and gravitate toward those with solid forecasts and consistent performance. Reducing uncertainty increases value, and companies that can demonstrate reliability will always command a premium.

Hidden Drivers of Real Value

It's fun to be able to talk to your buddies about all the revenue that your business does and then portray that you have a $100 million business. It's a vanity metric among US business owners. But if that big revenue number doesn't translate into transferable value, and if you don't have the systems, people, and positioning to support it, it's just revenue.

Customer base is one value lever you can pull, but it's not the only one. While companies may talk in terms of revenue or cash flow multiples, buyers are also paying for the investment you've made in your team, your processes, and your technology.

Those "soft" areas are often the real value drivers, yet they're the most misunderstood. Many owners assume top-line growth equals value. It doesn't. When growth isn't supported by strong infrastructure, it destroys value rather than creating it. Revenue at all costs kills valuation.

One of my favorite old *SNL* sketches is Phil Hartman's "Citywide Bank of Change." The bank's entire service was converting money into different denominations: $20 into two tens, a $10 bill into fives, or even quarters if someone wanted. The customer finally asks, "How do you make money doing this?" and the straight-faced answer is: "Volume. The more change we make . . . volume."

We joke in the office when we're busy but not actually creating value is, "Are we having a Citywide Bank of Change moment?"

Making change isn't valuable. Yet business owners do it every day. They chase revenue for the sake of revenue. They stay busy. They create movement. But none of it improves valuation, scalability, or long-term strength.

Chasing revenue at all costs kills value. If you're focused only on top-line growth and ignoring the investments that make that growth *transferable and sustainable*, like process, talent, technology, and positioning, you will never capture the highest value for your business.

The Subscription Model Transformation

We know that the subscription model is wildly attractive to future business buyers. If you can switch somebody from a "when I need you" model to an "I'm just paying you all the time" model, it doesn't get any better than that. Set it, forget it. I spend $13.99 per month for Paramount+. I haven't turned Paramount+ on in a year.

To service a subscription model, you must make certain investments in how you schedule proactively. You might need to overstaff a little because you never know when you're going to be needed if it isn't an on-call situation.

We helped an HVAC service company go from per-job pricing, where all their revenue came when it was really hot or really cold, to a flatline subscription model. That evened out their cash flow, but they had to increase their spending because they needed to make sure that they had low employee turnover. They needed to make sure that they had the resources available for consistent, proactive maintenance, scheduling, and planning—all those things that weren't reactionary but were proactive.

Turning their business from a reactionary to a proactive model also helped with their employees. The employees knew that they would always be busy, not just when it got to 110 degrees in Portland, Oregon. It changed the way that they looked at what they were doing. They weren't just there to fix something; they were there to keep things working.

From an employee perspective, that mindset shift is enormous. They have a lot more ownership in the game. They get better feedback from the clients because they're not just solving problems. They're proactively participating.

Most of their technicians had never been in a world where they were trying to be proactive, so they had to be trained. They invested in systems that didn't have them just responding to calls, but going out, building relationships, and showing up on a Thursday to change the filters and check in on their clients. It was not a responsive thing. It was a forward-looking, proactive system for managing customer service that took more people, different systems, and more training for the techs.

Being proactive with your business is not without risk. If you just switch to subscription-based revenue without providing a unique value proposition for your client, they're probably not going to stay with you forever. Eventually, they could do the math and realize they didn't need to pay you each month; they could have just paid you one time.

You have to create value based upon the things that you can lead with intention and think, *As a buyer, what would I want to buy into?*

Culture Is a Currency

While culture doesn't necessarily show up as a line item in your cash flow or your income statement, it's there. It's driving these things.

You can take a pretty regular business, inject a culture of ownership, customer service, or innovation (whatever is important in your industry) and build value in just as great a way as increasing your revenue, cash flow, or documenting your systems.

One of my favorite examples of value through culture is Zappos. They weren't doing anything revolutionary; they were selling shoes, something people have done forever. The only real shift was selling them online. But what made them unforgettable was their extreme commitment to customer service.

The CEO empowered customer support to do whatever it took to make people happy.[1] Sometimes that meant simply helping someone choose shoes. Other times, it meant spending hours on the phone talking through their needs. Legend has it that one call famously lasted nearly eleven hours. The duration wasn't the metric of success. The point was empowerment. Employees felt ownership, and customers felt seen.

Zappos built loyalty so strong that customers wouldn't think of buying shoes anywhere else. They sent flowers, helped people shop competitor websites when Zappos didn't have what they needed, and treated each interaction as relationship-building, not transaction management. That level of service created *stickiness*, and stickiness is a massive value driver. In retail, where contractual recurring revenue is rare, repeat customers are gold.

This kind of culture doesn't necessarily pay off immediately in dollars. But over time, Zappos could point to repeat-customer rates two or three times higher than industry competitors. That retention multiplier translates directly into valuation.

Employees also loved working there because they weren't handcuffed by rigid scripts or time limits. They had autonomy. That led to lower turnover, a hidden but powerful value driver.

Most calls were normal. But the legendary stories, the moments when

---

1   "About Us," Zappos.com, accessed February 1, 2026, https://www.zappos.com/c/about; Richard Feloni, "A Zappos employee had the company's longest customer-service call at 10 hours, 43 minutes," Business Insider, July 26, 2016, https://www.businessinsider.com/zappos-employee-sets-record-for-longest-customer-service-call-2016-7.

someone went above and beyond, became part of the culture, which trans-ferred into marketing.

Some leaders would be terrified to allow their teams that kind of free-dom, but Zappos proved it works. Brand loyalty. Customer lifetime value. Employee retention. A differentiated culture. Those are the things that make a company worth more than just the products they sell.

That's why codifying culture matters, not as a buzzword but as embedded values and behaviors that survive leadership transitions. Zappos grew into a case study in culture-centric business strategy. And ultimately, Amazon acquired them for $1.2 billion. Not bad for a shoe store.

Once you're clear on your value drivers and on your unique proposition and how it ties to daily behavior, you start seeing how culture supports financial independence and long-term valuation, not just short-term sales.

Key Takeaways

- **Identify your value drivers.** Ask what daily actions make you stand out from competitors and align with your core values.
- **Audit your time investment.** Ensure every hour spent con-nects directly to returns you demand as an investor in your business.
- **Double down on differentiation.** Once you know what drives value, lean heavily into those elements in your strate-gic planning and forecasting.
- **Avoid head-to-head competition.** Instead of competing directly, amplify what makes you uniquely valuable in the marketplace.
- **Measure your competitive advantage.** Track how your dif-ferentiators translate into measurable business returns and premium positioning.

You don't need to compete head-to-head with everyone else in your market. Instead, lean into being yourself—and being more of yourself. That differentiator becomes a competitive advantage that generates the returns you're seeking. As Sally Hogshead says, different is better than better.[2]

So you figured out what drives value. Now it's time to assign a number to it. You're going to set your target stock price. And you're going to treat yourself like you've just been listed, even if you never plan to go public.

---

2   Sally Hogshead, *Fascinate: Your 7 Triggers to Persuasion and Captivation*. New York: Harper Business (2010)

Part III

Operate Like You're Listed

CHAPTER 8

Set a Stock-Price Target, Even If You Never Go Public

What if you listed your business on your own private exchange and started looking at your business like you've just gone public, answering to all your different investors?

Picture the big, beautiful day where you stand on the balcony of the NYSE and ring the opening bell, celebrating all the successes you've had in business and where you're going in the future. You're able to be listed because you have targets and a plan for the future.

In this chapter, we're going to set your target stock prices for your business. Where is it going to move? What are the bold things you are going to do to maintain this long-term focus and increase your stock price, even if you never plan to have an IPO and ring the opening bell?

Market-Cap Mindset

We help clients set their target stock price. When they look at it in pure per-share value, they start thinking like investors, not just founders or CEOs. "I'm at $25 a share today, and I need to get to $35 a share in the next five years to support my financial independence."

When we start talking about the smaller metrics of defining a valuation target, we start asking different questions. We start talking about the trade-offs we need to make, the investments we need to undertake, and how to structure what we do every day to align with those goals.

If you don't know where you're going, any road will get you there. You're looking for specific growth that aligns with your key value drivers and the exit stock price you've been dreaming of. Without a clear lens on your company's valuation, you can end up on so many different paths.

Reverse Engineering from Your Target Valuation

You have to define your valuation target and then reverse engineer your decisions from it. You choose that target based on your goals and what you think the business can actually do. Then every quarter, you update your stock price and ask, "Did I hit that target of where I wanted to be at this point to get where I need to go at the end?"

When we set those targets and start thinking about the steps to get to the next place, it helps align everything. That's where the forecasts come from. That's why you're doing this work: to get to that ultimate stock price increase. If you were buying a publicly traded company, you would expect its leaders to have plans on how to increase the value of the stock. Come up with your own ticker and list yourself on your own index.

If you're running your business like it's already public, then you value forecasting and double down on your unique value proposition, accountability, and investor-grade thinking to make sure you're doing the things that increase value every day.

The Power of One Metric

When I did this for myself, I discovered that when I could distill success down to one metric, I gained a lot of clarity. I've either increased or decreased the value of my business. We just talked about having a one-page sheet with three or four metrics. What if we could distill it down to just one metric—the value of the business?

A perfectly clean stock price doesn't exist on the open market, with all the extraneous factors of the NYSE. But if you're looking at whether the things you did and plan to do are moving an individual stock price, it feels different. It provides a level of clarity around all your decision-making. All those other things support it. But at the end of the day, if your stock price isn't increasing and you're not getting the returns, you're probably making the wrong decisions.

We're employee-owned and conduct a valuation every year. We know our stock price. If I'm not looking at what I'm doing every quarter with an outside valuation bent, if I'm not tracking our value drivers and making decisions that would impact that stock price every month in the long term, I'm letting my team members down and not increasing the value of the stock they hold.

It is the same for the employees. They understand that they own shares at a certain price and the things they do every day have an impact on that. This makes them want to find better ways to do things operationally.

Employees bring ideas to the table because they know that if they increase the key value driver—in the accounting world, that's cash flow—they're able to increase the value of their business. In our business, revenue and free cash flow are our two numbers. We know we need to do things to support both. We also know that our people are our number-one assets. These are our value drivers.

What if we all have a common language around everybody doing better? That shows up in the stock price, the accumulation of all your efforts appearing in the value.

One powerful benefit emerges: It gives you a clear target while creating increased ownership and accountability across the board in a productive way. You feel accountable to your employees as a leader, and it drives your decisions. Your employees, in turn (especially in an employee-owned company), see what they're working toward. Because they want their share value to grow as well, it guides their decision-making. It's a mindset change from the most entry-level employee to the person at the top.

We're not chasing eight different metrics. At the end of the day, we're chasing one. A publicly traded company's CEO is judged on the performance of their stock price. Period. All the other numbers matter, but that final number doesn't lie. It provides clarity and direction.

When you can see the impact of your decisions and plans on that ultimate exit, on that ultimate share price, it accumulates. It brings together all the other ideas you've been working on.

Strategic Patience with Your Stock Price

We've had periods when we knew we were investing back in the business and that it wouldn't be immediately reflected in the share price. For our firm, we know that most professional services firms grow their share prices during periods of acquisition. We purposefully stepped back and said, "We need to get better at acquisitions. We need to be more targeted and structure the firm so that when we do them, we're going to crush them. These are going to be the best acquisitions we've ever done."

We took time to restructure the firm, redefine our merger targets, and develop a whole new approach. Did our stock price languish when we weren't actively acquiring? Yeah, we stayed flat, and it sucked. But we knew we were investing that time to do better so that our free cash flow, after we'd bought or merged in these other companies, would be stronger in the long run.

Once business owners understand their stock price and what influenced it, everything becomes clearer. They stop chasing ideas that didn't move value and are more comfortable saying no.

Even my most experienced business owners benefit from tying decisions to something familiar like valuation. It cuts through the noise. It removes the emotional reaction to big offers or flashy stock movements and replaces it with a grounded benchmark: *How does this affect our stock price?*

Seeing that metric puts you in the same mindset as the companies you hear about on earnings calls or read about in *The Wall Street Journal*. It puts you on a defined path—not just operating the business but also building value.

Sometimes the stock price stays flat. Without context, that can feel discouraging. But when everyone understands the decision-making behind it—why growth paused, what investments are underway, what's temporary and intentional—that flat line isn't alarming. It's expected. It's planned. And the transparency reduces anxiety because nothing fundamentally changes.

Your core business remains solid, but you also know that *good* isn't the goal; *great* is. Growth requires intention. When you can explain where you are now, where you're going, and why the effort matters, people rally. In an employee-owned firm, that clarity isn't just motivating; it's personal. It's critical to understand how the work connects to value, to your future, and to why the next milestone matters.

Demanding Real Returns from Your Business

While you're on the path toward price targets, investors demand real returns at the same time. You deserve a return on your business because you're the one taking the risk, guaranteeing the debt, doing the work, and putting your capital on the line every day by owning this business.

Public CEOs can't hide behind just lofty valuations; they're told they need to provide return on investment. So should you. If you don't know what your earnings are compared to what you have invested, how do you know you're getting the right return for the risk you're taking?

This is where we apply financial rigor to stock prices and returns to see what you're getting, not just for the day-to-day work you're putting in but for the amount of investment you have inside your closely held business.

You need to know the metrics that show you're getting a real return. Take your net income and divide it by your number of shares outstanding. You get your earnings per share. It's more complicated for privately held companies than publicly traded ones, but this foundation changes everything.

But there's math for this. You can say that your collective efforts were able to return $20 per share. You can then walk over to the market and say that other similar businesses are only generating $15 per share. Or you might find that they're doing $50 per share in addition to having significant overhead from being a publicly traded company. What are you doing wrong? It's providing one of those crucial comparison points. If it's not to industry (because every business is different), you're comparing yourself to what you thought you would do for earnings per share.

Going through that process and knowing your earnings per share are going to make you a more educated seller of your business if that's a future possibility.

There's also a process to consider normalizing your earnings and understanding what happened in that period that may not happen again. That also helps with forecasting and looking out to the future.

Knowing your earnings per share and what you wanted them to be versus where you ended up is a crucial exercise.

Calculating Your Owner's Return

The next concept is owner's return. Public companies report not just what they earned but also how much value they return to shareholders. We bring that same thinking to private owners: *Here's what you earned for working in the business, and here's what you earned as an investor.*

When we express that return as a percentage of the company's value, it becomes meaningful. If your owner's return works out to 10 percent, that means all the risk, time, and effort beyond your wages produced a 10 percent return.

For context, maybe the S&P 500 returned 14 percent this year, meaning that financially, you might have done better letting your money sit in the market. Next year, the S&P might be at –8 percent, and your positive 8 percent will feel great. The point isn't to sell your business and go buy index funds. It's to evaluate the return on your investment with the same discipline you'd apply to any other asset. Ownership shouldn't get a free pass.

Many clients look forward to this comparison. They want to know: *Did I beat the market? Did I outperform what I projected? Am I doing better than my peers?*

Understanding your return changes how you view the business. It becomes the return for everything that comes with ownership: late nights, risk, guarantees, customer demands, employee management, etcetera. If we can't quantify that return, or if it's negative, then it's not a return at all.

The truth is that every business has a return number. Sometimes, that number isn't good. If your business isn't generating a return worth holding long term, then it's time to ask why you're doing it and whether something needs to change. This framework puts the risks and rewards of ownership into proper perspective.

Build Toward the Buyer's Math

Anyone can make you an offer, so you might as well do the work of building toward the buyer's math. Make sure you know the things about your business that would allow you to get the highest purchase price if you ever did want to sell.

Knowing your numbers matters. Future buyers want real returns—the dividend or distribution yield we just discussed. When you can calculate it, explain it, and prove it, your valuation increases.

Global strategy and transformation consulting firm Capgemini's acquisition of a software company is a great example. The potential acquisition didn't just have market share; the company could also demonstrate real earnings, real growth, and a track record of improving returns.[1]

Buyers pay for cash flow and the confidence that those returns will continue. If a buyer needs a 10 percent return and you can show consistent performance above that, you have leverage. You can justify a higher purchase price.

That level of confidence requires scrutiny, like tracking margins, returns, and the financial drivers you may not watch closely in day-to-day operations. The work now is building the case: not simply showing that you produced dividends, but demonstrating a rising stock price, improving performance, and increasing value over time.

You must reverse engineer the questions a sophisticated buyer will ask. If someone walks in with a major offer, what proof will you need to justify the number? What data proves future earnings—not hypothetical but documented behavior?

When Capgemini paid $3.3 billion, it wasn't because the business was worth exactly $6,076 per share on that particular day. It was because the company had already built a culture of demonstrating returns, not just estimating them. The value wasn't in speculation—it was in evidence.

If you want your business to be worth something, you must build something that somebody's going to want to buy.

---

1   "Capgemini to acquire WNS to create a global leader in Agentic AI-powered Intelligent Operations," capgemini.com, July 7, 2025, https://www.capgemini. com/news/press-releases/capgemini-to-acquire-wns-to-create-a-global-leader-in-agentic-ai-powered-intelligent-operations/.

Key Takeaways

- Define your current valuation and the valuation you're targeting.
- Make the target visible and understood across the organization.
- Use valuation-based language so that everyone aligns with the same goal.
- Evaluate every decision against its impact on future value.
- Apply valuation concepts specifically to your industry and business model.
- Track progress over time so that movement toward the number is tangible.
- Reject decisions that move the valuation backward, unless there is a compelling, strategic reason.
- Accept that staying flat may occasionally be intentional but never accidental.
- Treat valuation as your North Star—the filter for how you lead, invest, and grow.

Now that you know your number, everything changes. We're going to operate like we're listed. We're going to bring even more of that public-company discipline into your privately held business.

CHAPTER 9

Run Your Business Like You're Going Public, Even If You're Not

When private equity started getting hot and heavy in buying CPA firms, they began sending offers and wanting serious conversations with us. That's when it hit me: *Oh my gosh, we're not ready to be bought. We haven't done the things we tell our clients they need to do.*

You always need to be ready to sell your business.

Now we're going to look at how to apply the internal controls, transparency, and documentation standards public companies are required to follow, and bring those practices into your privately held business. When you do, you raise your company's value.

Even if you never plan to sell or go public, these habits make the business run better and prepare you for the day someone shows up with the kind of offer you've always said you'd consider, the true *F-you money* moment.

When we started getting calls from people interested in buying the firm, I went mentally through those due diligence checklists we have our clients complete when they're preparing to sell or buy another company. Then I thought, *If this private equity group sends me this list to go through, I can't answer all these questions for the firm I've worked at for the last twenty-one years.* That felt gross. Doctor, heal thyself.

We knew we had something incredibly valuable. We knew we had solid operations, amazing HR files, a great IT stack, contracts, and scheduled vendor relationships, but I also knew that we were vulnerable when it came to our clients' customer base. We didn't have all our clients' contacts, referral sources, and everything we did for them documented in any meaningful way.

We knew every tax and payroll tax return, all the compliance-based requirements, and everything else we needed to do for every client, but we didn't capture the spirit of all the other things we do for clients in our CRM.

The deep value of our company comes from our relationships. People would ask, "Well, who are your top ten largest clients, and what industries are they in?" I would say something like, "I don't know. I work with Bob." I couldn't articulate the true value of our firm, which of course was in our clients.

The Wake-Up Call: Operating Without Public-Company Discipline

We were not running with public-company discipline. I wouldn't say we were flying blind, but we were operating out of that quadrant of "urgent but not important," where all the deadlines are taken care of. We did what we said we would when we said we would do it, but that was it.

We weren't focused on building long-term value, and we couldn't truly demonstrate what our team was capable of. We weren't running the business as if anyone was watching. So we invested the time and energy to overhaul our CRM and engagement tracking systems.

Now every engagement, every client interaction, and every commitment is documented. We have signed scopes of work, visibility into future capacity by team members, and a clear forecast of next year's revenue. In other words, we finally did what we tell clients to do.

Was it expensive and painful? Absolutely. The team had to document everything while still meeting deadlines, and I understood why we had postponed it for so long. But that investment increased our value. It improved communication, created operational clarity, and made the business far more attractive, to us and to any future buyer. We even used our own due diligence checklist, the same one we give clients, and applied it to ourselves. We're not planning to sell. It just feels good knowing the business is built right.

Running like someone is watching means building systems that are repeatable, provable, and verifiable. In a strong internal-control framework, if it isn't documented, it isn't done. If someone can't retrace the steps, it doesn't count. It's not enough that the right signatures are on the checks—we need a system ensuring that the check was reviewed before it ever went out.

Run your business so someone else could step in, review the records, and confirm that what you *think* is happening is actually happening. That's how you build confidence, value, and a business that can scale.

The Immediate Payoff: Unexpected Benefits of Documentation

After we got over the shock of having to do all the work to get all our client relationships documented, a big benefit is that we're now able to onboard people faster.

When team members join our organization, they can see the whole swath of what we do and whom we serve. We're able to transfer the knowledge of how we operate more quickly, and we're not hunting and pecking for how we show up and serve each client. This system has transformed our client service because there's no more "This department does this, and you should go talk to somebody over there." Everything lives in one place.

The clarity we gained about our client base was equally revealing. You think you know your customers, but then you step back and discover patterns you missed. What felt like scattered clients—dentists, doctors, nursing homes—revealed itself as a concentrated 30 percent of our revenue coming from health care when we included physical therapists and medical-billing companies.

That knowledge changes everything: how you go to market, your positioning, your entire strategy. We confirmed our large contractor base and heavy concentration of engineers, but we also gained a new lens for targeting markets. The system has more than paid for itself, and while it was expensive, the new value is reflected in our current valuation.

This reinforces the point about building value, whether you plan to sell or not. It's about getting that financial independence.

The immediate internal benefits of comprehensive documentation are massive. When there's an emergency handoff, if someone has an unexpected medical procedure and someone else needs to finish their project, everything is documented: the five deliverables, the due dates, the client meeting schedule.

Before, it was all in people's heads (maybe three people's heads) but not repeatable. You'd find yourself calling someone who's out on leave, asking them to walk you through a project. If I told you I hadn't done that, I'd be lying. Usually, it was someone on planned leave who had to leave early, and you're scrambling to find where they saved files or what deadlines they communicated.

What's exciting is how this positions us for authentic AI integration. AI can only run successfully on what you feed it, so when you're well documented, it has a good diet to operate from, all in one place.

The Deal Killers: When Poor Controls Destroy Value

Controls create confidence. In the spirit of documentation and repeatability, if you don't have controls around your financial reporting, sloppy financials can kill a deal instantly. I've seen countless clients find a merger candidate or acquisition target. They love the projections, the people, and the story. They see the synergies and say, "Michele, go take a look at their books."

Then . . . I find that they're absolutely terrible. These aren't mom-and-pop shops; these are large deals with people who should know better.

Even if you don't know better now but want to go to market in two years, start getting your systems together.

I ask for five years of records, and they say, "Those first three years were messy, but we got our act together in the last two." Fine. But too often, the acquisition target says, "Those aren't our real books. We've had personal spending mixed in, and my cousin still works here, getting eighty grand a year." We can prove that out, but buried underneath is everything else: car payments, vacation expenses, condo costs.

I'm not backing all these personal expenses out. When forecasts are vague statements like, "We're going to grow by three million a year," that's not good enough. I need specifics. *What are the units? What's the measurement? How does it tie to operations? How did you achieve growth last year?*

When the books don't balance, the price drops, and the terms get ugly. Buyers want predictability and trust. When they ask me how the due diligence looks, I say, "It's an absolute disaster. Don't trust them." They're buying based on revenue only, paying out on collections instead of the up-front price the seller wanted.

Without tight controls, you're not just running inefficiently; you're exposed. Those tiny cracks, like personal expenses mixed in or improper revenue recognition, become deal killers.

"That second one sounds like a big crack."

The things I've heard would shock you: "I have a second set of books." I walked into a famous bar in our hometown that a client was considering purchasing. When I asked for tax returns, the owner said, "Those aren't my real numbers. We do mostly cash, and I don't report it."

I told him, "That's fine. You 'pre-took' your purchase price on that. We're not paying you for unreported income. You got that money tax-free. I'm not paying you for it twice. Whatever money you took is just that. Enjoy it."

"Well, that's not fair."

He took a major hit in the purchase price. This happens all the time. Sometimes it's not just the financial side; that's the easy one. As an accountant, I can talk numbers. But we had one investor whose target company had great books. Everything reconciled, everything tied out; there was solid forecasting—but no signed contracts for their major clients.

"They just renew every year."

"With us, will they renew? Do we have a five-year deal? Because you've told us it's a five-year deal, but you have nothing signed. How do I buy that?"

Or they're creatives with highly compensated professionals working without signed contracts. We'd be buying employees and team members who could leave and start their own businesses with no barriers at all, taking the value with them.

The Hidden Liabilities: Tax and Compliance Traps

Then there's the tax minefield most business owners never see coming: income tax, sales tax, and everything in between. A client hires a remote employee or starts shipping to another state and unknowingly triggers new tax obligations. They're not careless; they just didn't know. But when it comes time to sell, that ignorance shows up fast: "You've got a $300,000 sales tax liability. We're reducing the purchase price unless you want to absorb that risk."

One surprise like that can change the entire deal structure. That's real money left on the table.

Internal controls aren't bureaucracy. They're protection. Running a due diligence checklist every year helps you catch blind spots before someone else does. You don't have to fix everything—just know where the gaps are. Focus on what adds value or removes the biggest risk. Address what keeps you up at night. Then revisit the checklist every few years as the business evolves.

It's always better to know your risks than to be blindsided by them—better to deal with *known unknowns* than face *unknown unknowns* during an acquisition. Because when exit time comes, ignorance isn't bliss; it's expensive.

The point is that clean financials and strong controls don't just protect value; they influence deal terms, which can matter just as much as the price.

The Gold Standard: Acting Public Before You Are

Asana is a great example of doing things the right way early. They operated like a public company long before they ever listed. By building strong internal controls and transparent reporting, and creating thorough documentation ahead of time, they were able to pursue a direct listing on the NYSE. This allowed them to bypass underwriters, avoid costly road shows, and keep more value in-house.[1]

Their preparation meant they didn't need someone else to vouch for their credibility. Investors already trusted their financials, their brand, and their processes. The payoff was significant: no lockup period and no forced dilution for employees or early investors. Direct listings aren't perfect, but for Asana, the foundation they built made it possible and successful.

Importantly, they didn't wait until the moment they wanted to go public to start behaving like a public company. They built discipline early. They

---

1   Paayal Zaveri, "Asana, the hot productivity software startup valued at $1.5 billion, just filed to go public via a direct listing," Business Insider, accessed February 1, 2026, https://www.businessinsider.com/asana-productivity-filed-s1-to-go-public-via-direct-listing-2020-8.

embodied the idea of going public in private long before the bell rang.

Not every business exits through an IPO. Your "bell ringing" might be making a sale, completing a generational transfer, or stepping aside while someone else runs what you built. But the principle holds: Prepare now so you're not scrambling later.

Do the work ahead of time because, eventually, someone will look under the hood. It's better that they find something you're proud to hand off.

Key Takeaways

- Run a cost-benefit analysis of documentation and controls through a simple lens: If a buyer came tomorrow, what weak spots would keep you up at night?
- Conduct a self-audit, surface gaps, and prioritize fixes that add immediate value or remove the biggest risk.
- Adopt the "Run like someone's watching" principle by making processes repeatable, provable, and verifiable. If it isn't documented, it isn't done.
- Move knowledge from people's heads into systems (CRM, scopes of work, checklists) so that value doesn't walk out the door when people do.
- Recognize why documentation lags (practical constraints, high-trust cultures) and counter it with minimum required artifacts: signed contracts, clean books, control proofs.
- Convert high internal trust into "Trust but verify" for outsiders: ensure that third parties can validate performance without you in the room.

Reduce anxiety and increase valuation by preparing now so that diligence tomorrow is a nonevent, and terms tilt in your favor. Next, we'll explore funding options that protect your freedom, amplify your upside, and preserve the value you've built.

CHAPTER 10

Choose Funding That Aligns with Freedom, Not Friction

I've watched our clients bring on partners and sell parts of their business with dreams of increasing value, serving more people, and growing their legacy. But after taking on that equity and new partners (maybe without doing all the due diligence), their vision quickly gets sidelined. They're not enjoying what they're doing anymore. What they're running feels foreign to who they used to be and who they wanted to be.

You're bringing people into your business and letting them be part of your dream and your direction. What is that worth to you? How do you help vet it? How do you find capital structures that get you where you want to be while letting you keep control and your vision through that process?

That would be my worst nightmare, and it's hard to see, because no partnership starts with hope of failure. There's absolute hope for faster growth, a bigger future, and success on the other side. Sometimes, you don't need a partner to do that.

We're going to explore different ways to fund your vision, options that align with where you want the company to go and that don't compromise that direction.

Your capital structure matters: who owns your company, where your debt comes from, and the expectations tied to that money. When those elements match your values and long-term goals, you set yourself up for real, sustainable success.

Capital comes with a cost. That $500,000 you need to invest in your company to reach the next level could end up costing you $20 million.

Equity partners can feel like the easier path, especially when lending conditions are tight. But too many business owners underestimate the long-term cost of giving up ownership and future upside. Every share you issue today represents value you won't fully benefit from tomorrow—not just financially, but in control, direction, and strategic freedom.

This isn't only an early stage issue. Mature businesses seeking capital for growth projects often overlook how expensive that future equity really becomes. Decisions made under pressure can permanently alter the trajectory of the company.

Before bringing on partners, understand the true cost of capital. Compare giving up ownership to simply taking on a loan. Most importantly, ask yourself what control, vision, and long-term autonomy are worth to you.

The Credibility Advantage: Building Trust with Lenders

If you run your business like a publicly traded company, your cost of capital goes down.

When banks and nontraditional private lenders can trust your financials because you've done the groundwork, they'll lend to you at better rates. You won't need to seek private equity or strategic partners where you're giving up not just interest, but equity in the business as well.

We worked with a business owner who needed $500,000. They were in a rough spot and knew they needed that investment in machinery to take on new projects coming their way.

The traditional financing route meant going to a bank for $500,000 with immediate payback requirements that didn't align with cash flow. But banks and private lending institutions will work with you, offering payment deferrals without requiring equity.

This business owner chose an alternative, which was to agree to a deal for another company in town to buy a percentage of the business for $500,000.

Those contracts he invested in equipment really took off. He landed Google and other major clients. He went from a $5 million company to a $20 million company. That $500,000 stake went from being worth $500,000 to a massive $2 million slice of a $20 million exit when private equity came calling.

He could have paid 8 percent on $500,000 for five years and owned his entire company free and clear. Instead, he gave up 4 times more than what he could have borrowed at 8 percent.

Sometimes giving up equity feels like less friction: no begging banks, no loan committees, no payback schedules. There's math surrounding the cost of capital, whether you choose equity or debt.

There's no one right answer for every situation, but the only way you can secure aligned capital is by assessing both options and building a strong case when you approach banks. When they can trust your work, partners won't need as large an interest in your business.

The math is stark: 8 percent on $500,000 for a few years versus giving up $2 million in equity value. That's the difference between strategic financing and costly desperation.

When they exited, that partner who took a risk eight years prior simply went along for the ride. He took a significant risk when the company wasn't in great shape and deserved his reward. But did the client understand that he would lose $2 million of his exit price when the same funding was available on more favorable terms elsewhere?

Understanding your true cost of capital isn't just about math; it's about preserving the future you're building.

Designing Strategic Partnerships That Protect Your Vision

When taking on investors or partners, you can either dilute your mission or deepen it, depending on how you design the deal.

If you decide that $500,000 is better raised from a strategic equity partner, alignment becomes critical. The moment someone joins you as an owner, especially if they have access to your team or influence inside the business, you must ensure that they fit your culture, support your vision, and won't complicate decision-making.

Taking on an equity partner requires structure. Define the relationship up front by clarifying boundaries, outlining decision rights, and documenting how you'll operate together. Whether they're silent or active, expectations must be explicit—not assumed.

If the value of that partner is strategic, hold them accountable for it. Ask for introductions, revenue opportunities, hiring support, or any other role they're meant to play. Ownership alone doesn't automatically mean engagement or benefit.

Many owners assume, *He knows everyone in the industry, so this will pay off.* The question is: Have you discussed what that looks like in practice? What's the plan? Trust—but verify.

Equity can accelerate growth, but only when everyone is aligned and working toward the same mission with a documented road map.

This isn't a "money in, welcome aboard" situation. You need standards. You need boundaries. Both sides deserve clarity on expectations, responsibilities, and outcomes. Misalignment is where partnerships fail—not in the legal documents, but in the unspoken assumptions.

Those expectation conversations are just as important as the contracts. They create freedom.

If you can't both articulate what you agreed to in one clear sentence, you're headed for (using a Thomas the Tank Engine reference) *confusion and delay*.

The Partnership Paradox: Scaling Together or Falling Apart

Taking on a business partner is like a marriage: easy to get into and incredibly difficult and expensive to get out of.

Business owners bring on strategic partners to fuel growth, not just for money, but also for alignment, energy, and leadership. The upside is synergies. Some partner stories have amazing synergies. Think Warren Buffet and Charlie Munger . . . that worked out pretty well.

The risk is misalignment that fractures the business, the friendship, and the reputations. Bringing the wrong partner on doesn't just slow you down; it can destroy things you've worked decades building. The right partner can make things really click.

The solution is a rigorous evaluation process before you sign anything. There's a model for how to decide whether you should take somebody on as a partner: talking about your vision, values, expectations, roles, and authorities. At the exact same time you're talking about legal structure, you plan your exit.

Everything ends. Through death, through sale, through "I want out." Unless you want to end up with that partner's spouse as your new partner, you need to have your exit terms planned. You do not want to be talking about your exit after you've already built something big; it makes it much harder to negotiate how somebody's getting out of the business.

When Handshake Deals Destroy Everything

Two entrepreneurs launched a million-dollar venture on nothing more than scribbled notes on what I call "Big Chief yellow tablet paper" (not even a real legal agreement). Just raw enthusiasm and an LLC filed in Kansas in under two minutes. They pooled resources, bought buildings, purchased equipment, and opened bank accounts. No partnership agreement. No defined roles. Pure excitement driving the ship.

Then one of their spouses got sideways with the other spouse.

Everything unraveled. They had to tell everyone it didn't work. The lawyers descended like vultures, writing their own narrative about who deserved what in the absence of any clear agreements. Litigation. Broken friendships. Lost momentum. All because they skipped the hard conversations on the front end.

I hate hard conversations too. But here's the brutal math: Four hours with a shared attorney could have created a bulletproof plan beforehand. Instead, they each spent two hundred hours with different attorneys, trying to figure out how to screw the other person out of the deal. That's an additional cost in time wasted, not counting the $150,000 in legal bills, which exceeded the actual value of their partnership. Insane. All because they skipped the hard conversations.

When you bring on partners, you're not just giving up a slice of the pie. You're surrendering infinite possibilities to misalignment. I get excited when running with scissors. I love the rush of partnership deals and the intoxicating vision of what we can create together. That's exactly when you need someone saying, "Let's not get too excited. Maybe we should do the due diligence. Maybe we should get some legal documents drafted."

If you can't balance yourself, get advisors who can guide you through that process. Because what happened to these two was devastating. They both lost significant time, money, and momentum. Nobody deserved the destruction they received.

The hidden advantage of initiating these uncomfortable conversations is that if the other person balks, you know there's a problem right away.

You're done. It's better to discover that incompatibility now, not after you've built something together.

Think of it like a prenup. While you're caught up in wedding excitement, discussing divorce feels gross. But what are the odds this won't work? About 50 percent. Just as likely to fail as succeed. Business partnerships? I don't have exact percentages, but I'd bet they're worse.

A well-crafted prenup or a well-designed exit agreement don't predict failure. They let you function at the highest possible level, knowing you're protected if the unthinkable happens.

During the partnership, you don't have to worry about the exit. You've already talked about it. You can just work on the business and the relationship.

The Mailchimp Model: Choosing Independence Over Speed

Mailchimp is a great example of alignment and discipline. The two founders bootstrapped the business from day one and repeatedly turned down venture capital, not because the money wasn't available, but because they didn't want investors dictating timelines, strategy, or priorities. Their core value driver was customer loyalty, and they believed deeply in spending money to acquire customers and take care of them, not cutting support to chase short-term margins.[1]

Could they have grown faster with outside capital? Maybe. But by reinvesting profits and staying 100 percent founder owned, they kept control, avoided dilution, and eventually benefited almost entirely from their $12

---

1   Vihanga Himantha, "Bootstrap to Billions: How Mailchimp's 'No VC' Strategy Built a $12B Exit (And When to Say No to Money)," Medium.com, June 11, 2025, https://medium.com/@vihanga.himantha/bootstrap-to-billions-how-mailchimps-no-vc-strategy-built-a-12b-exit-and-when-to-say-no-to-11b0d0o6d2bb.

billion sale to Intuit. They built the company their way, at their pace, with no outside pressure to exit before they were ready.

Could aligned investors have helped them scale sooner? Possibly. But they didn't believe those investors existed—not ones who truly understood their model or would protect their philosophy. Venture capital would have pushed them to cut the very things that made Mailchimp valuable. So the founders stayed focused, ignored distractions, and built a company meant to last, not just scale.

When your vision and capital structure are aligned, everything becomes clearer. You stop chasing opportunities that don't fit. You stay the course. Clarity makes the choice and the outcome far stronger.

Key Takeaways

- Define your objective for the capital infusion: What outcome must it fund (e.g., capacity, customer acquisition, margin improvement, resilience)?
- Decide your trade-offs up front: What are you willing to give up, and what is nonnegotiable?
- Align funding with mission and long-term goals: Only choose bank debt, silent investors, or strategic partners that won't pressure a pivot away from your core strategy.
- Learn the pattern: See *The Founder's Dilemmas* (Noam Wasserman) for start-up trade-offs; apply with extra caution in mature companies where you're risking a valuable future.
- Run a cost-benefit analysis for every relationship: bank, silent investor, business partner, etcetera. Quantify the financial cost, control concessions, covenants, and exit implications.
- Sanity-check your mindset: Don't let the excitement of "getting the cash" or a shiny partner blur the true cost of capital and control.
- Simple rule of thumb: If cash flows are predictable, prefer

debt. Consider minority equity only when strategic value is explicit and control is contractually protected; if neither condition is met, wait.

The next step is to clearly think about how you reward and engage the people who help you build and continue to build the business.

We're going to talk about how employees, when they have skin in the game, can accelerate the growth of a business and how we can do that without losing control. We can model some of the ways that publicly traded companies are able to do that in our privately held businesses in a much nimbler way.

CHAPTER 11

Give Employees Skin in the Game Without Losing Control

I'm not speaking to you as a consultant with the things that I've seen with employees having ownership in a company. I'm speaking to you as a person who runs an employee-owned company. And I've seen firsthand how our people outperform traditional CPAs and traditional consulting firms. I've seen how our revenue is more, our employee turnover is less, and the engagement that we get from our team members is just so difficult to replicate in any other way. They own the outcomes because they actually own the business. And I promise you, this works.

In this chapter, we're going to talk about how to share the upside with your team in a way that deepens commitment, builds their wealth and yours, and preserves control for you, the business owner, so that everybody wins.

Why Public Companies Use Equity

Equity isn't just a perk or part of your benefits package; it's a performance strategy.

Public companies use equity awards through incentive stock options and restricted stock to align employees with driving shareholder value because they become shareholders. They get to participate. It drives long-term thinking behavior and helps these companies compete for top talent at a different scale, offering various levels of future ownership.

Without equity-based incentives, what are you trying to do other than pay higher wages? Eventually, compensation taps out. You can't just keep paying people more and more. A wage or bonus structure doesn't necessarily endear somebody to the net income the business generates. People are personally engaged only in what they get to take home.

Let's take a page from that public playbook. We're going to use equity as both glue for our stickiest employees and fuel for having them think like owners and make decisions like owners. We can increase our value while we increase theirs.

The Proven Performance Advantage of Employee Ownership

Deloitte studied S&P 500 companies with employee stock-purchase plans. Companies that gave employees opportunities to purchase stock and participate outperformed their peers in nearly every long-term metric. Their shareholder return, cash flows, and revenue growth all outperformed peers. At the ten-year mark, it was eighty-one basis points higher than companies without these plans. Most of these companies ended up on best-places-to-work lists.

Reinforcing that we all share in the financial upside of our efforts drives performance and loyalty. We all know employee turnover is incredibly costly, and keeping the right people helps build the best places to work.

With shared upside making your employees stickier, your business becomes worth more because employee turnover is less. It helps align your team members with their goals and their commitment to those goals.

This completely realigns workers' relationships to their work because they have a stake in the outcome. They care beyond just the transaction of "I provide labor; you provide wage."

Instead of a transactional relationship, we're now in a long-term wealth-building relationship together. It's a deeper commitment. It's more fun. The us-versus-them mentality isn't necessarily there.

When goals, key results, and the direction of the company are shared openly, everyone understands how their daily work connects to where the business is heading. They also understand that once the organization reaches that destination, their financial reality will change as well.

I spent five years at the largest accounting firm in the world. When I worked harder, the partners became wealthier. I might have received a slightly better bonus, but I knew they were building significant wealth based on the leverage of their team. We would attend holiday parties at their impressive homes and see firsthand what our work created for them. I am not opposed to partners becoming wealthy. The real question became this: How do I justify benefiting from my team's efforts if they never share meaningfully in the value they help create?

You can structure things to allow more of that alignment.

Let's not create friction with the people working with you to build value for everybody. There are powerful ways to address this and really build a value-making machine.

Because the people who are your partners, the people making you the most money, the people who just paid for your pool are talented enough that one day, they're going to realize how much they're making you. And that they're not getting any of it. And that they don't have to stay.

The newer generations understand the delta on this a lot faster. They're more willing to take risks. They want a leadership place at the table. They don't necessarily want to pay for equity stakes and write big checks to have a seat at the table. They want to do it through how they're showing up every day for their job. They want an opportunity to grow with you. We can design plans to address that, even when we're not public.

Phantom Equity: Creating Owners Without Giving Up Control

Phantom equity has real impact. We help our clients develop phantom equity. It helps their key team members start to understand what it's like to be an owner. They aren't just participating in their wage; they're participating in the net income and growth of the business. The decisions they make every day feel like they have real financial stakes.

It helped start that key group of managers for possible real equity in the future. When people understand how the business makes money, they make smarter and more strategic choices. Without this upside, that top talent might do it on their own and build it without you.

We've helped our clients offer skin in the game for their employees through phantom equity, stock appreciation rights, or compensation triggers that don't dilute control. You're not actually giving up ownership of your business. You're developing compensation plans that mirror the upside of being an owner.

When we do these phantom equity plans, we build them into your business, rewarding people in a way that's meaningful while teaching them to think like owners.

In some of these phantom equity plans, we tell the employees what the owners allow into the plans: *When I sell this company, you will get X percentage of the net cash of the sale.* When owners talk about building for an exit or looking for a white knight bringing F-you money, employees aren't scared. They'll get to participate.

At its core, a phantom stock plan is a compensation arrangement. You're not taking on a partner. They don't have any say. They don't have to vote. They don't have to guarantee debt. They get to start learning the business. They may take distributions at a similar rate to you for the percentage they own in the plan. It starts to build them into owners so that they can understand where they're headed.

A lot of our clients will say, "I'm going to make a 10 percent shadow equity
pool." Then they'll say, "I have two people who should be in that pool.
You're going to own 6 percent. You're going to own 4 percent. When I take
out distributions from the net income of this business, you two will be getting those payments as well. And when we go to sell, 10 percent of the net
proceeds are going to you guys." We don't have to buy it back from them
when they want to leave. It's a compensation plan. It goes on their W-2s.
But if the business doesn't make money, they don't make money.

So many compensation arrangements are based on the top line. *Bring in the
revenue. Do the things. Once we hit this, we'll revenue share.* I need them to
focus on the net income and cash flows of the business.

"Revenue at all costs" is a model, but it doesn't make sense for a ser-
vice-based model. You can't keep promising revenue share when you're not
boosting that bottom line, that net profitability.

Testing the Waters: When to Transition from Phantom to Real Equity

When do you shift from phantom equity to real equity? Whenever you're
ready.

Phantom equity is a useful testing ground because it allows you to begin
sharing information without giving away ownership. You can share balance
sheets, income statements, forecasts, and cash flow. The team begins to
understand the business at a deeper level than they did as project managers or department heads, and you get to watch how that information
affects behavior.

It also shows how people react when there is no payout. With phantom
equity, a bad year means that they receive nothing. With real ownership,
a bad year may mean putting money back into the business. Seeing how

people respond in those moments tells you a lot about whether they are built for ownership or only for upside.

Phantom equity can also be a bridge to an employee stock ownership plan (ESOP) or a management buyout. It helps identify whether you can build a group of future owners, whether that is a handful of leaders buying your shares or the entire company through an ESOP trust.

For smaller companies or teams without strong leadership depth, I recommend starting here. It is a practice round. It builds financial fluency and alignment, and it prepares the business for a possible employee-owned future.

One of our contractor clients rolled out a phantom stock plan during a difficult year, and no one received a payout. Instead of checking out, the team leaned in. They focused on improving gross margin, cutting waste, and meeting more often to review financials and forecasts. They did this because now the numbers were tied directly to their personal financial outcomes.

That is the real purpose of starting with phantom equity. It lets you see who behaves like an owner before you make them one.

The ESOP Advantage: Creating Generational Wealth

An ESOP is a benefit plan that primarily owns company stock. When the company sells, everyone inside that plan benefits from the sale. They also benefit when they retire, as the trust buys the stock back and makes them a cash payment. Every year, hopefully more frequently, people watch the value of their ESOP stock grow and increase. When the company makes contributions, they watch it increase. When the stock price goes up, they get that money when they retire.

If the business sells to a strategic third-party buyer before they retire, they could receive an even larger amount in their retirement accounts. It creates generational, life-changing wealth, especially for long-term employees—just like Deloitte found that the payoff was eighty-one basis points higher after ten years. The ESOP isn't a get-rich-quick scheme—not for the people exiting and not for those in the plan. But it's more than just a plan. It's a culture that compounds along with your retirement balances.

I love an ESOP success story. My husband enjoys Fat Tire beer, and we have one of their bicycles mounted high in our garage. We bought it at a charity auction years ago. To me, it represents the success of an employee-owned company.

New Belgium Brewery, the Fat Tire guys, was 100 percent employee-owned before its acquisition. The myth about employee-owned companies is that they don't sell. This isn't true. Employee-owned companies sell regularly, and when they do, the proceeds go to the employees, giving them a real stake in the eventual full exit. Some ESOPs last forever and never sell, continuing to perpetuate ownership. New Belgium's leadership saw that they could achieve strategic alignment to grow faster. They chose to sell, and the profits went to the employees.

An employee owned, large, heavy-road contractor we work with sold in a small town full of hardworking, amazing people. This strategic sale created generational wealth change for families who had been working for the company. They received more money in their retirement plans, changing their life trajectories for retirement.

Hearing about an entire town, or a large percentage of people in that town, experiencing a generational shift in their financial situation is significant. These are asphalt layers making a good wage who would otherwise have to work until the age of seventy, then retire with Social Security. It's a fine life, but when they get an ESOP payout—one they don't contribute to as employees, one that costs them nothing—they have something they wouldn't have had otherwise.

Unlike a 401(k), they're putting the money away for you. They're letting you build equity in the business simply because you're employed there. We've seen this work at New Belgium and other companies. Even private equity firms like KKR now set aside 10 percent for employees through an ESOP when they acquire companies.[1] It's also super tax advantaged.

This is one of those moments when doing the human thing is also the profitable thing. When people participate in equity programs, they perform better and generate better returns for the business. Treating people well makes them care more, makes the business perform better, makes an exit happen sooner, or drives up valuation.

The alignment is incredible. The tax benefits are icing on the cake. When we help clients decide between an ESOP or a third-party exit, nine times out of ten, while they might get a larger dollar amount with the third-party exit on the top line, what they keep from an ESOP is typically a little more.

That sounds counterintuitive. From an outside perspective, you wouldn't expect to make more as an owner with an ESOP. But, when you sell to a third party, you're typically paying the highest tax rates because they buy your assets, that 39.6 percent highest tax bracket. Even if we stretch it out over time, when you sell to an ESOP, the tax advantages fundamentally change the equation.

Key Takeaways

- Ask yourself: *How do I create alignment between myself and my team members who are helping build this business?*
- Examine where your actions may be out of sync with your stated values and commitments to your team.
- Recognize that creating team alignment strengthens both current performance and long-term business value.
- Adopt a collaborative wealth-building mindset—view success

---

1   "Investing in an Ownership Culture," KKR, kkr.com, accessed February 1, 2026, https://www.kkr.com/approach/ownership-cultures.

as something you build together with your team, not in opposition to them.

- Understand that authentic alignment with your team becomes a unique value driver that enhances your business's attractiveness for potential exits or public offerings.

We now have our team invested and our capital stack. This last chapter will tell you how to memorialize and build a business that buyers want, even if you never want to sell.

CHAPTER 12

Own a Business That Runs Without You

Nobody goes into business to build something that dies with them. People start companies to make change, create a legacy, and generate wealth. But for that vision to outlive you, you must build something repeatable and transferable.

Too many business owners discover this truth too late. They reach the end and try to sell to employees who lack the knowledge or ability to run the operation. They approach competitors who take one look and say, "Why would I buy you when I'll just take all your clients when you're done?"

That's the worst kind of rejection.

It happens all the time, and it hurts because it's true. The result? Too many owners close the doors, wrap it up, and walk away with nothing. Maybe that's all they were ever going to be. Or maybe they simply failed to invest in making their business transferable and sellable.

Some people, like those lifestyle business owners who know that the odds of transfer are low, don't care. But beginning with the end in mind, building with intention to create something that transcends you and carries your important work forward without you, provides 99 percent of business owners a much more meaningful transition into financial independence and retirement.

Where do you think your employees will go when you're not there? To your competition.

The inverse strategy: Build a business your competition would be honored to buy—begging to buy. They should kill for your intellectual property and want your brand to replace their tarnished one.

One of my clients ran a casket-distribution company. You need real courage to work in death every day; it gives you a whole new perspective on life. They knew their suppliers were literally waiting for them to die so they could absorb the business, eliminate the middleman, and capture more profit.

The ironic part wasn't that the suppliers were waiting for them to die financially. The suppliers kept tightening the screws, while my clients stayed loyal instead of adding service lines, picking up different distributors, or buying funeral homes (all moves that could have strengthened their position). They remained faithful to the distributor who squeezed them.

Eventually the owner died, and his son died a couple of years later. The distributor bought them for far less than they had been worth a few short years before. Now the family legacy is gone.

Legacy becomes identity for business owners. When that identity faces extinction, they won't retire and won't sell, and they sometimes ride their company into the ground when they should have sold earlier. It's not about cash flow or employees; it's core to who they are. Separating those elements can be brutal.

I built a business where I know confidently that if something happens to me, this operation continues. My team is prepared, we're employee owned, and my legacy is secure.

The peace of mind is extraordinary, and that feeling is available to every business owner willing to build beyond themselves.

Let's make your business buyer ready, not just because you plan to sell but because you plan to transfer a business that leaves a legacy of resilience, and even joy.

Designing for Succession

Publicly traded companies are built to survive leadership transitions, and that durability is a major part of their value. CEOs change, but the systems, reporting, and culture stay in place so that the business continues without disruption. When there is continuity and predictability, investors are willing to pay more. We have all seen public companies with leadership turmoil, and the volatility shows up instantly in their stock price. Stability commands a premium.

If your business cannot thrive without you, it cannot scale, and it is not sellable. This is where you step back and ask what must be built so that the company and its legacy outlast you. Public companies are valued not only on performance but also on the reliability of that performance and their ability to repeat it consistently.

Strengthening leadership, upgrading systems, and creating resilience across the organization are investments. They require developing your management team and institutionalizing the way the business runs. But that is the path to a business that performs at the next level, with or without you at the helm.

The Lifestyle-vs.-Salable-Business Decision

Build to sell. You may not have immediate plans to exit, but building your business like you will makes it better.

Perform a critical analysis between whether you have a lifestyle business that you want to invest in for current returns or a salable, transferable business.

A lifestyle business is built for personal income and flexibility, which are not bad things. In a lifestyle business, you might not invest in some things because they may not be able to be institutionalized, repetitive, and transferable.

If you're building a sellable business, you have a true asset with systems, teams, and processes—so that if you take a two-week vacation, the business keeps going.

Both lifestyle and salable businesses can give you a job you love. Only one gives you a business from which you can exit.

I've seen high-revenue businesses with lots of employees where the goodwill is never transferred from the founder to the company. It's still about them. If that founder leaves, the company no longer gets the big contracts. It's screwed. That happens in huge businesses doing millions of dollars, but the owner doesn't do the work to take it from him to the next person. So it doesn't have value. It's a lifestyle business that supports a lot of people. That's cool, but transferability requires intention and investment just as much as increasing value.

Breaking Free from Hero Mode

If the business depends on you, it dies with you. Sometimes I see business owners who won't invest in transferring their personal goodwill to the business because it's part of their identity and they're constantly operating in hero mode.

As a business owner, you solved all the problems when all the problems were yours to solve. You didn't have a choice. You worked in hero mode.

Now, you must change the way you look at things: delegate, document, systematize, let people make mistakes, and build a capable team.

Codify who you are, what your legacy is, what the culture is, and how you do things. I'm not just talking about documenting how to make a deposit. I'm talking about documenting how you run meetings and how you talk to clients. Be willing to bring people into the rooms with you to let them start transferring some of that goodwill from you to them.

You have to make it replicable and not just relational. This feels wildly vulnerable because you're going to bring people into your baby and ask them to emulate what you do.

You must accept that you're planning to no longer be the person running these things. You're also moving from your core skill set—your knowledge and talent—to doing tasks you might not know as well: documenting, training, supporting. You're assuming an entirely new set of behaviors.

Your team won't do it perfectly. They might do it better. They might do it wrong. Either way, they'll learn.

Even if you never exit, this mindset can make operations smoother and allow you to step away. If you don't intentionally exit, maybe it will provide you with systems that help make everything run smoother.

I can create financial statements with my eyes closed. I can review an audit and tell you what's wrong with it. That's my wheelhouse. But writing a book? This is hard.

When I'm documenting and bringing team members in, I let them explain something to a client. Sometimes I think, *Those are words we don't use.* I can't step on them in front of the client in the meeting. When this happens, the failure is on me as a leader. I haven't talked about the *why* enough, how we explain things to clients. Maybe they need to observe five more times. It's so hard, and I'm much happier doing the things I've always done than reaching further and pushing harder into something uncomfortable. That's human nature.

It's vulnerable, awkward, and not always effective. Eventually, bringing team members in gets better but not without bumps along the way.

In the early stages, I thought if I lost a client, my personal income would drop. I'd have let a team member down. *Would I have to let people go?* That fear is real.

The fear from when you were starting your business and doing everything yourself doesn't go away when you say other people can do this. It's a hard mindset shift. But I can cast a vision that says it's better on the other side. A lot of people have gotten there, and it's good. You have to keep investing in it, though. Keep investing your time in building that team—the systems and documentation for things you didn't even think needed systematizing—so that you can step away (whenever that day may come).

From Burden to Breakthrough

We were helping a client who said, "You know what? I'm done, Michele. I want out. Time to sell." I told him, "You say that every three years, John. Let's do this differently. Let's get ready to sell. Tell me your pain points, because they will become your buyer's pain points unless they have a magic wand to fix whatever you have."

He said, "I'm sick of being the one who oversees the financials. I'm sick of being the one who talks to the bank and writes checks when there's a problem. I never know what's really going on."

I said, "What if you invested $60,000 to $70,000 in somebody who could take that off your plate and just bring you reports? Right now, you're not growing, but you have plans for growth. You'll make $60,000 less this year, but you won't have to deal with that. What do you think?"

If he sells to a larger company, they'll already have financial systems. If he sells to team members or someone else, they need that person anyway.

"All right. Fine. I'll try it. You're going to need them anyway for due diligence when you transfer."

"I've told you to invest in this for a long time. Let's just do it and see how it goes."

Was it hard? Yes. Did he spend more than $60,000? Also yes. Was he happy when he could step away and that financial burden was taken from him? Undeniably yes.

He felt lighter knowing he didn't have to worry about day-to-day financial stuff, and it made his business more sellable.

That investment allowed him to look at his business differently and gave him emotional freedom. He had to open his books to somebody and say, "Here's how we spend; here's what we do. Can you help me?" What had always been part of his identity (knowing the money), he let it go. He's happy; he hasn't sold yet, but he's building his management team to be ready to buy it.

When you asked him what was wrong, he knew specifically what was wrong, and it was all related to the money side. There was an emotional shift that had to happen first. He had to feel comfortable opening his books to somebody else.

Could it have gone badly? Sure. The person he picked to run the financial side could have let him down. That's why you must keep investing and supporting that person. Build a competent team around them. It's not just one person taking this off your plate. It's not "Set it and forget it."

You're going to have to do this work, no matter what. But ask yourself: Do you do it now, put in the hard work, and then have a system running? Or do you put it off and have to do it poorly, in a panic at the end?

The Power of Process and Systems

Process is a power move. McDonald's didn't scale because it had the best burger. It scaled because every burger was the same, no matter which location customers visited. They understood their value proposition: consistency. Their franchises were not just restaurants. There were operating manuals, training programs, controls, and systems that guaranteed a predictable product and experience.

Ritz-Carlton operates on the same principle through its Gold Standards. Their focus is not on micromanaging tasks like how to fold a sheet. Their system trains and empowers employees at every level to deliver exceptional service. At Ritz-Carlton, the customer experience is institutionalized. It lives in the culture, not in any one leader's head.

If a business relies solely on the founder's memory, charisma, or involvement, it isn't scalable; it's a bottleneck. Your systems for delivering value must be treated as strategic assets. They need to be documented, taught, and reinforced so that others can execute without you.

McDonald's scaled because leadership transitions did not disrupt operations. Ritz-Carlton scaled because the brand experience is consistent everywhere. When the system remains stable, the value remains high.

This is more than documenting financial procedures. It is building repeatable systems around what makes your business special so that it runs well into the future. That is how you protect the brand, preserve value, and secure your legacy.

When Systems Save the Day

I met a father whose son has special needs. His son's diagnosis is still unclear, and even the clinicians can't place him neatly into one category. While staying at a Ritz-Carlton on vacation, the family had a difficult interaction with a staff member who didn't understand the child's behavior and became authoritative and tense. Eventually, the situation deescalated once the staff member realized what was really going on.

Later that day, the father received the standard Ritz-Carlton guest survey. He responded honestly. He said that normally he would have written something angry, but this time, he tried to communicate with both honesty and compassion.

Within thirty minutes, the general manager and members of the hotel team were at their door with thoughtful gifts. The GM spent time playing with the boy one-on-one and arranged childcare services so the parents could enjoy a night out. The response completely shifted the family's perception. The company made a mistake, but what mattered was how they showed up afterward.

I have seen this myself. We are not luxury travelers, but I save my Marriott points and trade them in for Ritz-Carlton stays because the experience is different. During a family trip to Vail, my teenage son took a bad fall while mountain biking. We walked him back to the hotel, scraped up and shaken. Before we reached our room, four Ritz employees had already checked on him. A doctor called within minutes to confirm that he was okay, then showed up to examine him, clean his wounds, and ensure he didn't have a concussion. They sent supplies to the room, and both the doctor and general manager checked in again that evening and the next day. All of it was complimentary.

No one asked for help. No one filled out a form. Their staff was trained and empowered to act. That is what builds loyalty—not through perfection but in the way a company responds when something goes wrong.

That is culture in action. It is systemized empathy. And it is the reason customers stay for life.

Key Takeaways

- Identify which parts of your business couldn't function without you, then ask yourself why you're holding on to them.
- Recognize that building a sustainable business requires transferring your skills, knowledge, and processes to others from customer service protocols to your unique way of discussing the business.
- Examine whether fear (not logic) is keeping you from delegating. Sometimes, the barrier is as simple as being afraid to

show someone your books or share what you earn.

- Understand that perceived control often isn't real control—holding tightly to certain tasks may give you a false sense of security while actually limiting your business.
- Consider the paradox: By refusing to give up control of small things, you may be surrendering control of your business's ultimate fate and longevity.
- Ask yourself: "What control must I release to gain real control?" because clinging to minor tasks can prevent the growth and continuity your business needs to survive. If you don't bring people in to build a business that lasts without you, one that can transition, you're building a problem for whoever inherits this business.

The saddest thing for me is when I see it happen to the spouse who inherits a business that isn't built to last without the spouse who died. There is no transition plan, no succession plan, and we just carve it up. The last thing a grieving spouse needs to be doing is figuring out what was going on in this business. It's heartbreaking. It happens all the time. Even to the most well-meaning people, it happens.

You made it through. But we're not done yet. We need to reflect on what we've talked about, see what's worth your most immediate investment of time, and think about the kind of legacy you want to leave. Because you're going to leave one, regardless.

Conclusion

Now you understand what it means to think like an investor and expect
real returns from your privately held business. You know how and where to
invest so that you, your family, and your employees can move toward financial independence. When you apply these principles, you build a business
you enjoy today and a legacy you will be proud to leave. You have the tools.

Stop operating as if you work for the business, constantly reacting to problems and bureaucracy. Shift into building true wealth and a transferable
company. You now know what the public markets require and reward. There
is no reason to expect anything less from your own business.

Think like the market. Set your targets. Measure real returns. Demand performance. From this point forward, your business works for you and contributes
meaningfully to your net worth. That was always the goal. You did not start
this journey to own a job. You started to build something bigger.

Believing that you are making progress is not enough. Now you can prove it.
With the right metrics and rhythms, you will know exactly what your time,
money, and effort are producing.

The goal is not perfection. It is awareness. With awareness, you make decisions grounded in data, aligned with your values and long-term direction.
That is all any thoughtful leader can do.

I hope this process has helped you let go of the idea that your business
is small or static. You do not need to invent new frameworks. You can
borrow from the public markets and apply their discipline to your private
enterprise.

You deserve returns that exceed the time and risk you have invested. Building an advisory team accelerates strategy, strengthens decisions, and expands what is possible.

Accountability and reporting are not extra work. They create clarity and allow for faster, more aligned decision-making.

Failure becomes information. Success becomes a blueprint. Inside every business are unique value drivers that can be leveraged to maximize a future exit.

Long-term wealth creation follows the same path the public markets use: Define your stock, understand your stock price, and set targets and demand yield. Prepare now for the moment someone makes the offer you have always hoped for.

Surround yourself with the right banking partners, strategic partners, and employees who strengthen value rather than dilute it. Bring your team along. You can share opportunities without losing control.

Build the systems so that the business runs without you. Step back. Lead. Protect your legacy.

And when you are ready to operate like a publicly traded company without ever going public, visit gopublicinprivate.com.

We serve founders who are serious about scaling, who usually have between $5 million and $150 million in annual revenue, and who want outcomes and returns, not just income. We help leaders like you demand more from their business and gain peace of mind in the process.

You don't need to implement everything at once. Choose the pieces that support where you want to go next and start there. Just begin . . . and keep going, doing the next right thing.

Acknowledgments

I am well aware that my ideas have a habit of becoming other people's problems—often sooner than they'd like—whether at work or at home (see: my annual "thirty-ninth" birthday party planning). I don't underestimate the burden that creates. Big ideas are rarely tidy, and they're never carried alone. This book exists because many people were willing to help turn those ideas into decisions—and those decisions into something real.

First, to my clients: Thank you for trusting me with your businesses, your families, and your futures. Your questions, skepticism, ambition, and candor shaped this work more than you may realize. Every conversation sharpened my thinking, and every hard discussion reinforced why this perspective matters. Many of you have become trusted sounding boards and mentors, continuing to challenge and evolve my thinking.

To my SSC colleagues—thank you for the debate, the pushback, and the shared insistence on doing things the right way, not the easy way. Many of the ideas in this book were tested, challenged, and improved long before they ever reached the page. You consistently push me to think better and be better. And on the harder days, the laughter—and the hugs (especially from you, Chris)—matter more than you probably realize.

To my friends who raised the bar and refused to let me settle for comfortable thinking, thank you. You reminded me that better decisions—not more activity—are what create real leverage. Your influence shows up throughout this book.

Most importantly, thank you to my family.

My dad is the original thought partner behind much of what appears in these pages. A visionary leader, he had the foresight to incorporate employee ownership into a CPA firm long before it was fashionable. More importantly, he led with faith, integrity, and an unwavering belief that business should serve people—not the other way around. He taught me how to work with clients in a way that actually mattered and how to trust God while still doing the hard, disciplined work. His love for his family and his employees and his faith in Christ shaped more lives than he would ever admit.

My mom shaped this book in quieter but equally meaningful ways. Using her marketing background, she helped a group of CPAs show up as real, relatable people—no small feat. The small "**C**lose **P**ersonal **A**ttention" sign she designed for our office in the 1990s still captures the culture of SSC today and how we show up for our clients and each other. Her steady head, sharp instincts, and perfectly timed wit shaped how I relate to people every day—and occasionally remind me when I'm overthinking things.

My husband, a business owner himself, is always the first person "impacted" by my ideas. Your patience, kindness, and can-do attitude shape both our family and this work more than you know.

And to my kids: I wouldn't have attempted this book without your encouragement. Watching your curiosity and generosity, and how you show up for others, strengthens my faith and gives me hope for the future. I can't wait to see what you create as you grow and how you use your gifts in the world. Someday, I hope to grow up and be more like you.

And finally, to the reader: Thank you for being willing to think differently about your business. My hope is that this book helps you look at your work and your days with greater clarity—and make decisions with more intention and confidence.

About the Author

Michele has spent over two decades inside the businesses that matter most—privately held companies built by owners who pour everything into them and deserve real returns for it.

She started her career at the world's largest CPA firm, working alongside publicly traded companies. She saw firsthand how the systems, discipline, and investor-grade thinking that drive billion-dollar valuations actually work. Then she brought those tools to Main Street.

Today Michele leads SSC CPAs + Advisors, an employee-owned firm, and works alongside the team at Merit Financial Advisors—helping owners grow their business value and their personal wealth at the same time.

She doesn't just teach these principles. She runs her own organizations by them every single day.

Michele is based in Kansas, where she lives with her family and continues to advise business owners nationwide on growth strategy, valuation, and successful transitions.

For additional tools and resources, visit gopublicinprivate.com
or reach out to a gopublicinprivate@gmail.com